THIS BOOK BELONGS TO

Kipra Odoffer

START DATE 9/7/23

< On the opposite page, write the names of everyone in your
group, committing to pray for, learn from, and study with
them. For the next seven weeks, these will be your companions
as we journey through our study of Covenant.

Published by Christ's Church of Oronogo.
22145 Kafir Rd.
Oronogo, MO 64855

ISBN 9798856729886

Written by Elijah Dally
Designed by Lindsay Haddan and KaLisa Veer

◎ **Christ's Church** of Oronogo

🌐 CCO.CHURCH 📷❹▶ @CCO.CHURCH

Download the Christ's Church App available for iOS and Android.

YOU ARE NOT YOUR OWN

A SMALL GROUP STUDY ON COVENANT

TABLE OF
CONTENTS

SEPTEMBER 7 / SEPTEMBER 10, 2023

SERMON NOTES

Catch up or rewatch the sermon
from this week at cco.church/sermons

COVENANT GOD

SMALL GROUP LAUNCH

Covenants are extremely important toward understanding God. This is no doubt why the division of the Bible between old and new are followed by the word, 'Testament.' Testament is the Latin word for covenant, so when we say Old Testament or New Testament, we are actually saying Old Covenant and New Covenant. A covenant may sound like an archaic, strange word, but our hope is that this study redeems that. You see, God has made many promises throughout Scripture, and they find their expression in the form of covenants. The covenant provides the formal articulation of an exchange of expectations, goals of intimacy and joy, and the added assurance of their fulfillment. God uses these covenants not only to disclose Himself to others but to call others to Himself. This study will explore this idea and make it relevant to you. What promises did God make? What does it teach us about God? What does it teach us about ourselves? Covenants provide the framework for us to understand God's identity and for us to understand our own.

Now, this guide is not meant to be a substitute for the Bible but an aid to it. Like a greeter at the door, this guide is simply opening the threshold so you can easily pass through. So, it's important to lay out some ways this guide intends to do this.

First, this guide will walk you through what a covenant is and where we see it in Scripture. It's important that you don't skip this background, as it provides clarity for the rest of the study. As you explore the biblical theology of covenant, you will understand history in ways you never have before and develop a joyous expectation you never knew you could have.

Second, for each day of study, you will need a Bible, which can be a physical copy or one on your phone. You will use it to read each section of verses, asking yourself – what is God saying? Even in these grouped verses, there is a particular message. Once you've answered this, you can read through the devotional thought that accompanies each passage and work through the questions. There will be three of these a week, so pick three days and three times you can consistently dive in.

Third, pray. Let what God speaks through His word inform what you speak through your words to Him. Don't allow yourself to simply read this guide as information, allow yourself to engage the experience as a conversation. God tells us that He is uniquely accessible through His words to you, and in your words to Him – take advantage.

Fourth, have good conversation with your community. As you gather in groups, don't hold back from the highs and lows of this study. Share the blessings and the bumps. God also says He is uniquely accessible and present when we gather together in His name – so open up your heart and mind to the weekly gathering, and make it a priority to be there.

Lastly, this guide is meant to cooperate with the sermon series that will consider how our covenant God invites us to covenantal identity. This guide will build upon each week of our series and provide an opportunity for further study and reflection. Each week you will have space for notes which you can utilize during those messages.

A final note about the author – This was written by Elijah Dally, who serves as the Teaching Pastor at Christ's Church of Oronogo. Some devotions are written directly from his own life experience, but all the devotions were written out of a direct reflection on the text itself. They are written to engage your head, heart, and hands, and foster conversation that takes you beyond the guide itself. We hope this guide, and your study of covenants in particular, help you experience completeness in Jesus as we listen to His words and sit at His feet.

DISCUSS

1. What was the best thing you did this summer?

2. As your group begins this new study, what are some habits you want to cut out and some new habits you want to establish?

3. Determine what time of day will work for you to go through this devotional guide personally – set up an alarm in your phone that can act as a reminder to sit, hear, and speak with God.

PRAY

1. Go around and share one thing to praise God for and one thing to ask God for. Use the space below to write down what others in your group share.

2. Pray for the praises, petitions, and the start of this study.

WEEK ONE

COVENANT GOD

HEBREWS 6:16-19

People swear by someone greater than themselves, and the oath confirms what is said and puts an end to all argument. Because God wanted to make the unchanging nature of His purpose very clear to the heirs of what was promised, He confirmed it with an oath. God did this so that, by two unchangeable things in which it is impossible for God to lie, we who have fled to take hold of the hope set before us may be greatly encouraged. We have this hope as an anchor for the soul, firm and secure.

COVENANT BACKGROUND

Promises can feel like fragile things. They entail an exchange of expectations, defined by clear goals of intimacy and joy. To keep a promise will open a door toward all kinds of union, but to break one will produce isolation. Rarely will anyone make an explicit promise unless they are trying to infuse their words with a weight by which they themselves can be measured as true or false. Within a promise, there is an attempt to produce trust that a word spoken is an act completed, which is why Jesus is so specific in refining our words when He teaches in Matthew 5:37 that our "yes should be yes, and no should be no."

What's His point? Jesus is making us consider why we qualify anything with promise. Why can't every word we speak be infused with the weight of our own identity? The sad reality we have all come to know, either by our own lie or by being the victim of one, is that sometimes our words do fail. The act stands incomplete. Unions are broken.

A promise, then, becomes a way for us to provide extra weight to our words. To say, "I promise to..." is actually to say, "I really, really mean it when I say..." A promise is to add support to something that feels flimsy. And it feels flimsy, not because you think the person promising is an inherent liar, but because it takes one lie to make us mistrust the world, and the world is full of lies. The benefit of a promise is not for the one making it but for the one receiving it. A promise becomes additional assurance that what has been spoken will be fulfilled. The depth of the promise kept is correlated to the depth of union shared, but the opposite is also true. The breaking of promise is correlated to the depth of isolation and insecurity.

So why does all this matter? *Because God makes promises.* God provides, in our weakness and mistrust, the assurance of knowing that a word spoken by Him becomes an act fulfilled. In a world full of promise breakers, God wants us to trust Him as the ultimate promise keeper. How does God do this? The way God assures His promises is through the use of covenants.

So, what is a covenant? *A covenant is the bond by which promises are made, conditions are understood, and relationship is secured.* Now let's unpack that.

Imagine a wedding ceremony. Here a bond is in process; a union of lives. Once this ceremony is over, this man and woman will share all things together. They will share a name, a home, a family, wealth, and purpose. Every part of their life will be blended together so that neither is their own person – they belong to each other.

The essence of this bond is held together by certain promises made to one another (I, _____ , take you, _____ , to be my lawfully wedded spouse, to have/hold, for better/worse, for richer/poorer, in sickness/health, until death parts us), with certain conditions (adultery is a condition for the dissolving of this covenant, and faithfulness and love is a condition for great blessing and joy), and a ring is given as a sign of the covenant so that each person recognizes that this covenant has been secured (under God, by the state, and in the heart of the one giving the promise).

The questions we must ask as we look at the covenants in Scripture are drawn out from our definition: What are the promises? What are the conditions? How is our relationship secured? Is there a covenant sign to remind us? And what do all of these things tell us about the bond? What sort of relationship do we exist in? Some covenants exist because two parties agree to enter into one together, but others exist because a greater/stronger party has called a lesser/weaker party into it. The first is like a marriage; the second is like a parent/child relationship.

The point of all these questions is that they begin to inform both who God is and who He has called us to be in light of our covenantal relationship. What sort of bond do we have? What sorts of promises does God give to us, and we profess to Him? What conditions break or bless? Is there any way to be assured of union?

At every step along this path, we will find that the covenants create the story we belong to. The covenants start a redemptive history by which God reveals Himself as a holy, merciful, and loving God who has in mind to make a holy, merciful, and loving people. The covenant reminds us that something so significant has taken place that you are not your own.

The question this study and our sermon series hope to prompt is this: *Who do you belong to?*

'COVENANT' IS THE BOND BY WHICH PROMISES ARE MADE, CONDITIONS ARE UNDER-STOOD, AND RELA-TIONSHIP IS SECURED.

COVENANT WITH THE CREATOR

READ THROUGH JEREMIAH 33:19-26.

As you read, write down your observations and ask, *what is the purpose?*

There is a story of a magician named Phoenix. Phoenix was a master of illusion and attracted large crowds to watch him perform wonders. He could make large objects disappear, escape chains and locks, and even teleport objects from one space to another. There was one night in particular when Phoenix was going to perform a new trick that no one had seen before; he was going to make wood spontaneously combust into vibrant flame.

Now there is nothing magical about wood being burned, so Phoenix came up with ways to make this incredible: He had a clear tub full of water that he was going to put all the wood in, and to convince the audience it was, in fact, water, he invited someone up to drink a cup of it. Then he took the wood out and covered it with sand, and finally, he placed the wood on a safe surface made of glass so that everyone could see there was nothing being produced by what held the wood.

The crowd watched with anticipation, and the moment finally came. Phoenix gave everything he had to build up the moment of what was about to happen; then, he silenced the entire crowd. He came near the wood and put his hands out toward it, then he spoke those words as a support to his own 'power,' "Let there be light." The crowd expected to see an enormous roar of flames, but nothing came. Phoenix looked undisturbed and made a joke about stealing the words from God; he would use new ones, "Abra Kadabra!" The crowd waited, but nothing came. Phoenix looked uncomfortable, panicked. "Burn, I say!" he screamed, but nothing happened.

What Phoenix didn't know is that earlier that day, someone had accidentally deactivated the chemical meant to cause this combustion by bumping the small container that held it and releasing it to open air. Phoenix was dumbfounded, the crowd began to boo, and soon the curtains would close.

The reality of any illusionist, of any person, is that their words are always dependent upon something else. They require collaboration to have effect, which is why words can be such fickle things. However, there is one being whose words cannot return void, which always find their fulfillment – God. This power can be seen in those words Phoenix tried to steal, "Let there be light." The very syllables of God always activate reality because God depends on nothing; quite the contrary, everything depends on Him. Every word for God becomes promise because every word finds its completion.

This power to complete is what this passage in Jeremiah is referring to when God speaks to Jeremiah about the assurance he can have. God has made a lot of promises throughout Scripture, which have been articulated through covenant – the covenant with Abraham, the covenant with Moses, the covenant with David, but a question still plagues the mind of every person involved: *What if God's promise fails?* The answer to this question means everything to the Jewish people, especially within the context of Jeremiah when they are living in exile, living in a land and culture that is hostile to them. Will God save them? Will He bring them to the land He promised them and bless them?

God then references the covenant He made with creation itself. *"If I have not made my covenant with day and night and established the laws of heaven and earth, then I will reject the descendants of Jacob and David my servant and will not choose one of his sons to rule over the descendants of Abraham, Isaac and Jacob. For I will restore their fortunes and have compassion on them."* (Jer. 33:25-26)

Does the Sun warm? Do the stars shine? God says that He has entered into relationship through His act of creation, and the stability of the universe is what comforts our assurance that when He speaks, it is never void, and His word is that He will restore their fortunes and have compassion.

Okay, now let's talk about this covenant with Creation. What is Jeremiah referring to? As Genesis opens, it never says a covenant was made; God simply speaks, and creation comes. Yet when we look at the story, we can see it possesses all of the elements of a covenant: a bond, a promise, conditions, and security.

We see that creation exists at all only because it is in a bond with the Creator, totally dependent upon God. This creation finds its climax in the forming of Mankind, who shares sacred space in the garden. The command and promise from God is to be fruitful and multiply; He has given us everything to enjoy and a world to cultivate. Yet there is one condition – *"do not eat from the tree of the knowledge of good and evil, or you will die."* (Gen. 2:17) The relationship was secured by the Tree of Life itself, that wonderful source of eternal life that gives perpetual access to God and His blessings. The Tree of Life became a sort of sign and seal of their covenantal relationship.

When God speaks to Jeremiah, He is referring back to the very beginnings of creation itself and God's covenant with all He had made. By doing so, He shows 1. The world hasn't stopped spinning, so there is no reason to question whether God can and will uphold His promise, and 2. Not even Adam's sin, which invited sin, decay, and destruction into God's world, will be an obstacle to God maintaining His word, and neither will ours. God is clear what that word contains – God will restore and have compassion. Within that promise, Christ comes for sinners to demonstrate God's great compassion and His wonderful power to restore.

1. Have you been impacted by broken promises?
   If so, describe how that has impacted your willingness to trust.

2. How would you articulate some of the promises God has made?

3. Be in prayer for this study that you would grow in your understanding of the promises of God and the blessings of hope and rest that they provide.

COVENANT GOD

COVENANT WITH THE KING

DAY TWO

16

As you read, write down your observations and ask, *what is the purpose?*

We recently saw that the book of Jeremiah reflects on the covenant with creation, and here we see the terms of this covenant becoming clear. One thing you will notice is that throughout Genesis 1, it says, "God said" over and over again, but in Genesis 2, it changes. The language is no longer "God said" but "the LORD God." Here in Genesis 2, we have a 'zoom in' on the story. Here we aren't just hearing about a transcendent God who creates out of nothing, but a personal God who shares His space and name: Yahweh.

You see, LORD is in all capitals because the English translations are trying to honor the Jewish reverence of God's name. Every time you see LORD in all capitals, it is actually the divine covenant name 'Yahweh' that God gives to His people, but to revere the name, Jews would not say it. Instead, the people of God would write 'Yahweh,' so it was clear, but when they would read Scripture out loud, they would say 'Lord' instead – yet when you see LORD, it is His name. So here we see a shift, a movement from the big creator God to the personal, relational God.

DAY TWO

You will notice throughout this passage that God is in charge. He makes, He forms, He plants, He takes, He commands. God is, in fact, Lord and King of the universe, which is why when God forms Man "in His own image," it is truly unique. Nothing in God's creation enjoys this special status. Everything else has its place, its operation, its kind, but Man is given a special status and responsibility – *"God blessed them and said to them, 'Be fruitful and increase in number; fill the earth and subdue it. Rule over the fish in the sea and the birds in the sky and over every living creature that moves on the ground.'"* (Gen. 1:28) Notice how God shares His own reign with Humanity.

This initial covenant with creation puts all things in a bond with its Creator, and here God promises great blessing for the part of this creation which will reflect God as His imagers and co-rule with Him. Humanity is to enjoy not just his work in the garden (as God created in six days) but the fruit and rest of that work with the creator God Himself (as in the Sabbath).

Every part of this world sings of the covenant King. It praises the goodness of the Maker and, by extension, all He has made. It operates according to a righteousness that is not based on the random will of a tyrant but the artistry of a maestro, each atom of creation dancing to a rhythm that glorifies its King.

However, there is a condition. One thing which will break covenant and expel Mankind from the garden. One thing which will introduce death and decay into that which is good – Man must not eat from the tree of the knowledge of good and evil. Upon this infraction, humanity will die and be separated from its source of life.

Yet this condition was not enough to keep Adam from unfaithfulness. Indeed, neither fear nor love kept him from partaking of the forbidden. The co-ruler attempts to usurp God's throne in an act of divine treason to promote his own rules of good and evil instead of enjoying the blessings of the Divine Maker. This ultimate crime would result in sin and death and the estrangement of all Mankind.

This covenant with creation would also be known by some theologians as the Covenant of Works, by which Adam failed to delight in God's commands and therefore died to them. It is in this story that we see God's promises both in their great beauty and wonder and also great severity.

How will God redeem Mankind from death without becoming a liar? How can the promises of God become our hope and rest when they contain death for the criminal? Here we find a tension in that the faithful covenant-keeping King we most long for simultaneously becomes that Whom we most fear.

Yet, God would make another promise. Despite the curses of ruin that would befall God's creation, God looks toward the deceiving serpent with one more curse and promise: *"So the Lord God said to the serpent, 'Because you have done this, "Cursed are you above all livestock and all wild animals! You will crawl on your belly and you will eat dust all the days of your life. And I will put enmity between you and the woman, and between your offspring and hers; he will crush your head, and you will strike his heel."''* (Gen. 3:14-15)

The story would have been over rather quickly, but here we see our good covenant-keeping King make another promise which would form the trajectory for a new covenant that would satisfy the old and provide life in a new – the Covenant of Grace.

ASPECTS OF A COVENANT

A BOND
A PROMISE
CONDITIONS
SECURITY

1 What does this passage tell us about God?
Does this add anything new to your thinking?

2 What does this passage teach us about Humanity?
To what extent does this seem true in your own life?

3 Pray and thank God that He pursues the faithless in order to bring us back into relationship with Him.

COVENANT GOD

COVENANT WITH GOD

DAY THREE

READ THROUGH GENESIS 15.

As you read, write down your observations and ask, *what is the purpose?*

I know, I know, these last couple of days have been a little heavy in content, but the story is so rich! We will conclude our week's devotion with one more drama that sets the stage for understanding our covenant God and His covenantal story. Then I *promise* we will go lighter.

For those less familiar, I encourage you to read Genesis 1-15, but if you recall, we left the garden because of Adam's trespass. Mankind went into exile, living in the wilderness. Even though humans continue to procreate and expand across the world, evil proliferated right along in them. The condition of Man's heart became so vile that God's justice and wrath could no longer be restrained, and the world was flooded. Yet God chose one man to sustain the human race, a new sort of Adam with the same mandate, *"Then God blessed Noah and his sons, saying to them, 'Be fruitful and increase in number and fill the earth. The fear and dread of you will fall on all the beasts of the earth, and on all the birds in the sky, on every creature that moves along the ground, and on all the fish in the sea; they are given into your hands. Everything that lives and moves about will be food for you. Just as I gave you the green plants, I now give you everything.'"* (Gen. 9:1-3)

A covenant was made with Noah, which confirmed the promise of Genesis 3:15 as God sustained the genealogical line which would bring about the Savior. A sign and seal was given, not through the Tree of Life, but through a rainbow hung in the clouds. God's promise? First, Noah and his family will be spared, and then that God will never again destroy the earth by flood (and will restrain Man's wickedness so He won't have to.)

Noah and his family were saved and fulfilled the covenant promise of increasing in number. New cities and civilizations emerged, one of which tried to build a tower to God. God saw once more that Man's heart was distorted, and although they were unified, they were unified against the Author of life. God disbursed the nations across the world, and when all hope seemed lost, God called a man named Abram (who would later be renamed 'Abraham') to become a new nation, His covenant people. God was taking one more step toward fulfilling that promise we saw in Genesis 3; the Covenant of Grace was taking form.

DAY THREE

The story in Genesis 15 vividly demonstrates the incredible grace and love of our covenantal God. The promise to Abraham was given in Genesis 12. God tells Abram to go from his country and people into the land God will give him. Abram will become a great nation, be blessed, and be a blessing – yet here in Genesis 15, Abram boldly, perhaps even foolishly, asks God to give him a sign that God will fulfill His promise. It's been years and years, and Abram doesn't even have one son, let alone enough to start a nation. God reassured Abram that his servant would not be his heir but that God would follow through on His promise and give Abram a son. Then it says, *"Abram believed God and it was credited to him as righteousness."* (Gen 15:6) God then enters into a covenant ceremony with Abram so that Abram would know God would follow through on His promise, and this is where it gets good; this is where we see pure grace – look closely:

1. God says bring me a cow, goat, ram, dove, and pigeon.

2. Then God has Abraham cut them in half (except the birds, they were too small). This separation was incredibly important to the ceremony because it became the terms of the covenant. The brutality of the scene emphasized the consequences of breaking the covenant – if you break the promises you make and compromise the relationship, *your punishment would be to be ripped in half.* Covenants are seriously heavy promises.

3. Then, the climax of the ceremony comes when both parties walk through the pieces with an agreement of the promises exchanged, but something happens – *Abram falls into a deep sleep, and only God passes through the pieces.* It was always expected that the weaker party would walk through, and sometimes the stronger and weaker party would walk through, but to only have the stronger party walk through is historically astounding and wonderful grace.

The significance of this ceremony can't be understated. The grace of this covenant can't be overstated. This covenant was the catalyst of God's Covenant of Grace to begin to overcome the Covenant of Works (or creation covenant). By walking through the pieces and excluding Abram, God essentially says, "Not only will I take on the consequences if I don't uphold my promises to you, but I will also take on the consequences if you don't uphold your promises to me."

Years and years later, when the seed of Genesis 3 and Abraham's child finally came (Rom. 4), a Son would be born who would bear the curse of sin and death. Jesus would take on the punishment of a covenant breaker. Jesus would be God's solution to the Covenant of Works–where God promised death to the covenant people, and Jesus is the beautiful result of God's Covenant of Grace–where Jesus both suffers the consequences of the first covenant in our place and delivers us the blessings of the second covenant through His resurrection. In Christ, our punishment is taken, our righteousness is given, and we enjoy covenantal relationship forevermore.

We belong to God. And Christ gives new signs and seals of this covenant belonging – the Lord's Table and Baptism. Each time we partake of these emblems, we acknowledge we belong to God and we belong to each other. Our covenant God has provided a bond where His promises of Spirit and grace lead to our upholding the covenant conditions and enjoying the assurance of our eternal inheritance in Him (1 Pet. 1:3-10).

The point of all this is that God is a never-lying, promise-keeping, faithful God who makes promises based on His pursuit to redeem a broken world and those who broke it. He is not just the God who keeps covenant for Himself, but in Christ, He keeps it for sinners, and in this way, God becomes both 'just and justifier' (Rom. 3:26).

We've finished our setup for the background of the covenants, and next week we will turn toward how this begins to impact our reality. More, of course, could have been said. Each week I will add articles for those wishing to 'go deeper,' but to sum it up, next you will find the Biblical covenants synthesized into the story of redemption. It is also important to note that this covenantal framework of Covenant of Works and Covenant of Grace is one of many ways to see how the Bible describes redemptive history and is not meant to be exhaustive or final.

PRE-FALL COVENANT WITH ADAM

Created in grace to enjoy the blessing of God and co-rule with Him. Adam rejected obedience and forfeited relationship and brought the curse of sin and death.

POST-FALL COVENANT WITH ADAM

A victorious Savior is coming (Gen. 3:15).

COVENANT WITH NOAH

Preserves the genealogical line of the Savior (Gen. 6:18), and preserves the world until He comes (Gen. 9:9).

COVENANTS OF
WORKS
VS GRACE

COVENANT WITH ABRAHAM

Outlines the line through which the Savior would come and a covenant people would be built (Gen. 15, 17).

COVENANT WITH MOSES

Reveals the character of God, the depths of sin, and uses the sacrificial system and tabernacle to point to a better one in Christ (Ex. 20-31, Heb. 8-10).

COVENANT WITH DAVID

Paves the way for the Savior, not just to come from Abraham, but from King David, and establishes an eternal reign (2 Sam. 7, Ps. 89:3).

COVENANT OF WORKS (CREATION)

COVENANT OF GRACE (REDEMPTION)

NEW COVENANT WITH

JESUS

Fulfills all that came before it (Lk. 24:27, Mt. 5:17, Hebrews, Jer. 31) – the entire New Testament has descriptions of how Jesus fulfills the covenants.

HOW JESUS FULFILLS COVENANT OF WORKS

Jesus is the new Adam (1 Cor. 15, Rom. 5, Lk. 3-4, Col. 1, Eph. 1-2) who is perfectly obedient and without sin (Heb. 2, 4), and by His active obedience secures the blessing of eternal life and assurance of enjoying the garden-city to partake of the Tree of Life for a covenant people (bride) (Rev. 21-22).

HOW JESUS FULFILLS COVENANT OF GRACE

Jesus is God-man, who is the offspring of Abraham (Mt. 1), the promised Messiah (Mt. 1-2 – and anywhere 'Christ' is said), the better Moses (Heb. 3) that traverses the wilderness and provides a more perfect law, miraculous healing (Mt. 4-8) and more perfect temple (Jn. 2:19, Eph. 2, Heb. 7-10, 1 Pet. 2, Rev. 21). God Himself takes on our punishment of covenant curse (Gal. 3:13, 2 Cor. 5:21) and sacrificial death (Heb. 9-10), in order to complete God's grace and redemption so that by faith (Rom. 4, Eph. 2) we can be in the New Adam (Eph. 2, Jn. 15, 1 Cor. 12, Rom. 12.) and given eternal life with God back in the garden-city.

In the Covenant of Works, Jesus is perfectly obedient and secures relationship with God. He lives the life we should have lived. In the Covenant of Grace, Jesus takes our place as sinner and dies the death we should have died. In His resurrection, Jesus overcomes sin and death, and by faith, we are united with Christ so that our punishment has been paid and our righteousness is secured.

REFLECTION

1   Define in your own words what the Covenant of Works and Covenant of Grace are.

2   What role does Jesus fill in the Covenant of Works?
    In the Covenant of Grace?

3   Pray that our relationship with Christ would continue to define our covenantal identity in Christ.

GOING DEEPER

WHY DO WE NEED A NEW ADAM AND NOT EVE?

It's important to recognize that when Scripture speaks of Adam as the reason for the downfall instead of Eve that Scripture isn't disregarding Eve. Eve, in fact, was the first person to take from the forbidden tree, so why is Adam brought up so much? The article below explains this concept, which is crucial in understanding how we can belong to Christ's life, death, and resurrection.

COVENANTAL VS. DISPENSATIONALISM

If you've ever had questions about Israel and its place with the Church, this audio, or written transcript, will be of great help. Christ's Church believes that Israel and the Church both belong collectively to the people of God and therefore see the Bible's redemptive progression through the lens of God's covenantal relationships. Those who consider Israel uniquely separate from the Church and inheritors of different promises tend to see the Bible organized into dispensations of time where God interacts with groups of people. Below is a link that provides a helpful summary of these views as you seek to go deeper in your understanding.

SMALL GROUP
ROUND TABLE

SMALL TALK

What was a meaningful promise someone made to you growing up?

GOOD TALK

What stuck out this week in the study?

What questions or thoughts did you have as you read?

REAL TALK

Do you tend to have an easy or hard time trusting? Why?

Has that impacted your relationship with God?

DO SOMETHING DIFFERENT

We live in a world of a growing mistrust of institutions and accreditations, where our environments are easily shaken by disease, disasters, and geopolitical turmoil. What we need and long for is the unchanging, stable rock on which we can build our lives, and God is that unchanging rock.

The promises of God have proven true over and over again, and our lives should be informed by the promises now extended to us in Jesus Christ – that sin and death have been triumphed over, and therefore eternal life is all that remains. Jesus promised to return to restore all things and that the Spirit would comfort and transform. May we pray, "Lord Jesus, come," even as we allow the Spirit to make that true in us today.

PRAYER REQUESTS

WEEK TWO

COVENANT PEOPLE

1 PETER
2:9-10

But you are a chosen people, a royal priesthood, a holy nation, God's special possession, that you may declare the praises of Him who called you out of darkness into His wonderful light. Once you were not a people, but now you are the people of God; once you had not received mercy, but now you have received mercy.

SEPTEMBER 14 / SEPTEMBER 17, 2023

SERMON NOTES

Catch up or rewatch the sermon
from this week at cco.church/sermons

COVENANT PEOPLE

IDENTITY

READ THROUGH JEREMIAH 31:31-34 + 1 PETER 2:1-10.

As you read, write down your observations and ask, *what is the purpose?*

I'm a Lion; I'm a Red/White; I'm a three; I'm an INTJ; I'm a DC; I'm a Taurus – there are no shortages of personality tests that promise to give insight into your authentic self or the key to unlocking personal awareness and growth. These tests can be fun, they make for good conversation, but at the end of the day, personality tests are often based on the new passing scientific fad in psychology (Color Code, MBTI, DISC) or the new passing fad of some mystic imagination not based on science at all (Astrology, Enneagram) which utilize generalizations that many see themselves in.

Personality tests are marketable yet fallible, but if they tell us anything about humanity, it is that we share in common the longing to "know thyself." Who am I? What am I doing here? Why do I feel this way? The question of identity has vast implications for our day-to-day reality. How we choose to work, play, have relationships, spend our time, and spend our money, are all based on an assumption of who we are, what we should become, and what will lead to meaning and happiness. So, what is the key to understanding our identity? I bet you guessed it – our covenant with God.

Every time a covenant is made, it drastically shapes the identity of each party. God's character is never changed, but it becomes uniquely applied to those in covenant with Him. The person's, or people's, identity is almost always drastically changed from who they were before. Adam went from clay to king, Noah went from one of many to the chosen one, Abraham went from husband to husband and father, Moses went from an Egyptian household to building God's household, David went from tending sheep to ruling a kingdom. So, what does the New Covenant in Christ tell us about our identity?

1 Peter says that God calls for a people out of every tribe, people, language, and nation and creates a chosen race, a royal priesthood, a holy nation – most importantly, *a people for His own possession.* We are God's. We belong to Him. This covenantal reality means that at the core of your identity is not a number, a letter, or an animal, but God himself. You have the name of God on you and His law on your heart. *"For this is the covenant that I will make with the house of Israel after those days, declares the LORD: I will put my law within them, and I will write it on their hearts. And I will be their God, and they shall be my people."* (Jer. 31:33)

The law of the old covenant made with Moses was a beautiful revelation of who God is, but it also acted as a magnifying glass of who we were not. The law was written on stones for all to see, but it had no power to change people on the inside. The New Covenant characterizes this differently. The New Covenant doesn't disregard the law but says it moves from stones to hearts. The law no longer measures us because now, we embody it. The law was once a nagging fitness coach, but now we are totally strong – how? Paul tells us in Galatians.

Paul reflects in Galatians that *"through the law I died to the law, so that I might live to God. I have been crucified with Christ. It is no longer I who live, but Christ who lives in me. And the life I now live in the flesh I live by faith in the Son of God, who loved me and gave himself for me."* (Gal. 2:19-20)

We live as those who embody the law not because we have finally achieved perfection but because we have received the person of perfection. We haven't ascended the ladder of morality – quite the contrary, we fell all over it. God Himself, who is goodness, descended the ladder and took up residence in us.

When Peter calls us a chosen race, a royal priesthood, a holy nation, he isn't doing so because we have the right status, wealth, skin, or morality, but because we have received the true humanity, the royal priest, the holy king - Christ. We have forfeited the things which the world offers for identity and received an identity in Christ, that *"you may declare the praises of Him who called you out of darkness into His wonderful light."* (1 Pet. 2:9b)

Our New Covenant identity affirms what God told Jeremiah, *"I will be their God, and they will be my people"* (Jer. 31:33c). The Bible alone provides the clearest window into our worst struggles and our greatest joys as we locate our "true self" in Christ and His ransom.

1 We often define ourselves by our worst decisions or best achievements – how would you respond to that, and which do you tend to dwell on?

2 What does your life in Christ tell you about your identity? (Use 1 Peter 2:9-10 and expand those ideas practically for you.)

3 Pray that God would help you prioritize your covenantal identity over every other.

COVENANT PEOPLE

BELONGING

DAY TWO

As you read, write down your observations and ask, *what is the purpose?*

In 2016, amidst the growing frustrations and hostility of our political environment, something happened that brought the entire world together: Pokémon Go. Now, some of you have never played Pokémon Go, and perhaps even some of you have never heard of it, but there is no doubt that in July of 2016, you saw more people outside than you ever had before. Pokémon Go was a game on your phone that utilized your camera to produce an augmented reality where you could catch the mythical creatures known as Pokémon wherever you were. In fact, the kind of Pokémon that would show up were often tied to your specific location (water, forests, electric plants, etc.)

This game became an instant success, rivaling some of the world's most popular apps and becoming one of the most downloaded of all time. Hours spent on the game exceeded that of Twitter, Facebook, Instagram, and many of the other time-wasters on our phones.

One of the many observations of the impact of this game was the growth in physical activity. Many would be out and about, in parks, downtowns, and neighborhoods, tracking down the Pokémon in an attempt to "catch 'em all." In addition to growing foot traffic, it also increased comradery. Neighbors, and even strangers, who had never and would have never spoken before, engaged each other, offering advice on how to catch Pokémon or where they could find the rarest creatures.

This all may sound juvenile, but Pokémon Go became a social phenomenon that lasted the entire summer. Articles from major news outlets took notice of this mobile game, which was somehow bringing people from all walks of life together amidst the growing political hostilities. It created a sense of belonging around a shared joy. But like every other passing fad, Pokémon Go has largely faded out of the social consciousness, leaving behind a gap of belonging that is waiting to be filled by the next social phenomenon.

But we don't have to wait. God's covenant provides a community to belong to, life to be shared, and a joy not based on a passing fad or temporary stimulant but the eternal reality of God Himself.

In Ephesians 2, Paul recognizes that there were two types of people in the world: Jews and Gentiles. Those that knew God, belonged to His covenant promises, and had hope, and those that did not. But Paul here is reflecting on something stunning – that those two people can both belong to the New Covenant in Christ.

The Covenant of Works made humanity estranged from God and each other. This estrangement is most clearly seen in the violence that begins to ensue between Cain and Abel. But when the Covenant of Grace starts to take form with Abraham, there is a promise within it, *"I will make you into a great nation, and I will bless you; I will make your name great, and you will be a blessing. I will bless those who bless you, and whoever curses you I will curse; and all peoples on earth will be blessed through you."* (Gen. 12:2-3) Here Paul is reflecting on the fulfillment of that promise – not only has Abraham grown into a great nation (the Jews), but now all people on earth are being blessed through Abraham (in the person and work of Jesus).

Here Paul says that this nation is now growing beyond nationality or ethnicity into a diverse group from every nation, tribe, people, and language, but it is doing so in Christ. Christ is our shared love, joy, and hope. He is what reconciles humanity together, but this is more than mere fandom. We don't all like each other because we are rooting for the same Messiah. More emphatically, Christ is where we find our very belonging and where we find we belong to each other.

DAY TWO

Ephesians says, *"You are no longer foreigners and strangers, but fellow citizens with God's people and also members of his household"* (Eph. 2:19), and that, because you are actually becoming an entity or structure of space in Christ, *"the whole building is joined together and rises to become a holy temple in the Lord. And in Him, you too are being built together to become a dwelling in which God lives by His Spirit."* (Eph. 2:21)

This means that our covenantal identity is shaped, not only by how we belong to God, but to each other. Each person in Christ shares a level of responsibility, accountability, encouragement, charity, and sacrifice, which enable that exchange of life together. Every part of our life must be viewed through, not just our own wants and desires, but God and those who make up His household, His Church. What a covenant identity means is that our engagement with the Church must take priority over every other engagement – sports, school, work – anything that competes with our loyalty, time, and participation.

The Covenant means we have assurance of our eternal belonging to God, but it also means that we share in a belonging to each other. We don't have to wait for Heaven to enjoy the benefits of that belonging; quite the contrary, Scripture teaches that this eternal city is breaking out in the world right now through the person and work of Christ (Eph. 2:19-22).

1 In what order do you tend to prioritize your relationships? How have you seen that impact your life?

2 What would it change for your local church to become more prioritized as a place of engagement, service, and sacrifice?

3 Pray that God would build up your church to be a healthy, vibrant community that would be a blessing to those in the Church and those in the world.

EPHESIANS 2:19-22

Consequently, you are no longer foreigners and strangers, but fellow citizens with God's people and also members of His household, built on the foundation of the apostles and prophets, with Christ Jesus Himself as the chief cornerstone. In Him the whole building is joined together and rises to become a holy temple in the Lord. And in Him you too are being built together to become a dwelling in which God lives by his Spirit.

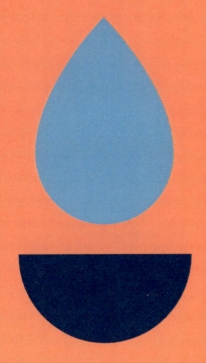

FAITHFULNESS

As you read, write down your observations and ask, *what is the purpose?*

When my son Dawson was three-years-old, he always copied his older brother. Whatever he saw his older brother doing, he would ask to join in. One particular spring that was baseball. Dawson would take his brother's bat and try to swing, but he simply didn't have the strength. He could barely hold it up, let alone have the control to carry it toward the ball. One time in particular, I put the ball on the tee so he could practice, but it just wasn't working. He'd miss everything or just smash the tee and cause the ball to fall off. He had no control at all. I would come up behind him and help him by grabbing his hands, showing him where to hold the bat, and then using my own strength to swing through that ball and make it soar. Dawson was attempting to accomplish this on his own, but the truth is what he really wanted was to make that ball soar, so when I came along to help him, he got the biggest grin on his face.

As Paul compares covenants in Galatians, he acknowledges this inner tension we all feel. There is this idea that we just have to be strong enough to resist temptation or do good things to earn our spot. If we just jump through the right hoops and try to be good, everything will be okay – but Paul has been using the entire letter of Galatians to explain that this way only leads to frustration. He is speaking to Jews and Gentiles who are having a hard time understanding the Covenant of Grace. All they know is that a covenant was established through Abraham and Moses, which had certain requirements: be circumcised, obey the law, practice Sabbath – but now Paul is coming along and saying that, while those things were good for their time, the Covenant of Grace through Christ is showing us something different. We couldn't be faithful to those things.

We were like Dawson trying to swing a bat and hit a ball without the necessary strength to do so. So long as you try to keep doing it the old way, you'll never actually exhibit the faithfulness to the covenant you think you are. In fact, Paul goes as far as to say that, so long as you keep trying to live under those old covenants separated from God's gracious plan, you are actually separated from the New Covenant in Christ.

Paul emphatically states that the only way to live faithfully to the covenant is not what you do but what the Spirit does in you. It is faith that both justifies you and therefore sanctifies you for a life of covenant faithfulness. You are in Christ, identified by His death and resurrection, and thus have become the space for His Spirit to dwell (Gal. 2, Eph. 2). Paul says that to receive Christ is to receive the Spirit which will produce in you what you could never achieve on your own; to receive Christ is to have the Spirit come, grab your hands, and provide the strength to make that ball soar.

The Spirit produces covenant faithfulness to glorify God and love our neighbor – not only that, but it produces every part of what makes our relationships with one another possible: love, joy, peace, patience, kindness, goodness, faithfulness, gentleness, self-control. Only through Christ and the Spirit do we become acceptable to God and solidified as one that belongs to His covenant people.

The challenge is that we still fail. We still feel the shame or guilt that comes along with that failure. Perhaps we even feel insecure about whether the Spirit is truly working in us at all. Where are we to find our assurance? Our security? It is in the faithfulness of God. Our salvation doesn't rest on what we do but on what Christ has done for us. If we have accepted what Christ has done for us, then we can be sure He is doing something in us.

These questions of whether God would be faithful to His promise (in this case, forgiveness and transformation) are not new. In each covenant, God gave visible words, signs and seals, physical symbols that would remind people of His covenant. For Adam, it was the Tree of Life; for Noah, it was a rainbow; for Abraham, it was circumcision; for Moses, it was the Sabbath. This appearance of a sign is why it is so important not to miss what Jesus says as He sits with His closest friends and gives them bread and wine, saying, "'Take and eat; this is my body.' Then he took a cup, and when he had given thanks, he gave it to them, saying, 'Drink from it, all of you. This is my blood of the covenant, which is poured out for many for the forgiveness of sins.'" (Matt. 26:26b-28).

This is why it is so important when Paul comes along and says, "In Him you were also circumcised with a circumcision not performed by human hands. Your whole self ruled by the flesh was put off when you were circumcised by Christ, having been buried with Him in baptism, in which you were also raised with Him through your faith in the working of God, who raised Him from the dead." (Col. 2:11-12).

The table and waters of baptism become the visible word, the sign and seal, the physical symbol, which communicates to us God's incredible faithfulness to save us from sin, but also His faithfulness to save us toward holiness.

"You are a chosen people, a royal priesthood, a holy nation, God's special possession, that you may declare the praises of Him who called you out of darkness into his wonderful light. Once you were not a people, but now you are the people of God; once you had not received mercy, but now you have received mercy." (1 Pet. 2:9-10).

REFLECTION

1. Do you currently ask for honest insight and discernment to grow? What areas do you need encouragement or accountability from your church to develop as a holy follower of Christ?

2. Describe what the table and baptism do as covenant signs in your own words.

3. Pray that the Spirit will continue to produce in you a life of faithfulness for God's glory, your neighbor's blessing, and your joy.

GOING
DEEPER

EXPRESSIVE INDIVIDUALISM

Expressive individualism has saturated every part of our culture. It is a part of our social imaginary, or in other words, it is the air we breathe. Expressive individualism can make it hard to understand how to belong to a group, especially one that belongs to God. Christianity does not call us to forfeit our individuality, but it does call us to recognize that it is only one part of our identity. Below is a link that will help you understand expressive individualism further, and what sorts of things to consider as we understand our role in God's people.

BAPTISM

Baptism is a concept that has different significance depending on theological tradition. Roman Catholics, Lutherans, Presbyterians, Baptists, and Independent Christian Churches (like ours) all have differing views on the purpose of baptism. At the QR code below, you'll find our church's understanding of baptism and its role within the Christian life.

SMALL GROUP
ROUND TABLE

SMALL TALK

What are you most passionate about that has community involvement (sports team, activities/ hobbies, music, etc.)?

GOOD TALK

What stuck out this week in the study?

What questions or thoughts did you have as you read?

REAL TALK

What does it look like for church to be a high priority?

How would you rate how true this is for you on a scale of 1-5, and why?

DO SOMETHING DIFFERENT

The Church, which is a people, not a building, is a visible manifestation of God's covenant community in the local body of believers you belong to. Christ's Church of Oronogo is one of these local bodies where we display and proclaim visibly what is true spiritually. We use Christ's Church as a unique home for God's believers to enjoy encouragement, accountability, and share life together, but this gathering is uniquely a church because it does these things through the Gospel of Jesus Christ and the revealed authority of Scripture.

Identity, belonging, and faithfulness are tied up into God's covenant people, and they are visibly seen through our engagement and investment in our local body of believers. We must strive to be invested and engaged at every level, not at the expense of every other activity of our lives, but in priority over those things. Make it a point to regularly serve, attend, and grow in your relational fellowship and knowledge of the Bible.

PRAYER REQUESTS

WEEK THREE

COVENANT HOME

COLOSSIANS 3:20-21

Children, obey your parents in everything, for this pleases the Lord. Fathers, do not embitter your children, or they will become discouraged.

SEPTEMBER 21 / SEPTEMBER 24, 2023

SERMON NOTES

Catch up or rewatch the sermon
from this week at cco.church/sermons

COVENANT HOME

COVENANT HOME

CHILD

DAY ONE

As you read, write down your observations and ask, *what is the purpose?*

From here on out, we get much more practical. God is not content to simply save you one day; His activity immediately begins to turn your world upside down, or rather, right-side-up. There is no such thing as being in covenant relationship with God and His people where it only impacts an hour on a Sunday morning. He demands all of you at all times, and this impacts the home.

This impact is undoubtedly why so many letters have explicit instructions for how God's covenant people should live in their relational environments. It is seen in 1 Corinthians, Colossians, Ephesians, 1 Timothy, Titus, 1 Peter, and the general use of the house metaphor to understand the life of the Church (1 Tim. 3:15).

We all have a unique family history that has formed us in unique ways. Those histories can be full of great joy or great pain. Paul's instructions are often meant to produce joy.

Now, a side note needs to be inserted here. I anticipate that, as we get into these new sections, the titles will make some people hesitant. I've heard many be frustrated when explicit topics are addressed and are often followed by, "I don't have children," "I'm not married," and "This doesn't concern me." My brother or sister reading this, we must graduate beyond the expectation that truth is only relevant when it serves our present condition.

This concern for wisdom is inherently a part of our covenantal relationship. Knowing what is good and wise is not simply so that we can live the best life in our relationship with God, but that we can help the family of God do so. To be in covenant is to recognize that you no longer belong to yourself. You belong to God. You belong to His people. Every part of what Scripture addresses is worth knowing because it helps us care for the family of God. God includes this material to bless His people, so drink from it and become the blessing God has called us to be. In fact, more knowledge of God's expectations for living in a healthy home could save many from having to endure a traumatic one. Certainly Paul has this in mind as he writes Ephesians.

When Paul addresses the people in Ephesus, he does so in ways that reflect on the promises given to Moses and the people of Israel. He says, "*Children, obey your parents in the Lord, for this is right. 'Honor your father and mother' – which is the first commandment with a promise – 'So that it may go well with you and that you may enjoy long life on the earth.'*" (Eph. 6:1-3) He is affirming what was said in the ten commandments, but Paul also points out that this is the only commandment that comes with a promise—if you do this, if you stabilize the home, "it will go well with you and you will enjoy long life on the earth."

So many principles could be brought out concerning children and the home, but I just want to bring out three:

1. Children are part of the covenant promise. Remember what God says to Adam? To Noah? To Abraham? *"Be fruitful and increase in number; fill the earth and subdue it."* (Gen. 1:28, 9:1, 15:5). Notice that both covenants agree that children are both great blessings, but also that children are how God intends to accomplish His promises. This work through children is why Paul can reflect on Exodus/Deuteronomy and remember the promise attached, *"It will go well with you."* In fact, **this is the only command in the ten commandments that has a promise attached to it.**

2. A child's obedience supports a healthy family. The structure of family relationships provides the boundaries for healthy interaction. When God provides the command, "Honor your Father and Mother," Paul follows it up in the New Covenant with, "Children, obey your parents." This obedience is good for the relational health of the family. This relational health is good for the health of society.

    Families form the backbone of every civilization – so goes the family, so goes the society. What this means is that we should not have a laissez-faire attitude toward parenting. Parents shouldn't lessen their expectations of their kids or outsource them to be shaped by school, sports, or any other community. To outsource discipleship is to give our kids to a different standard of virtue and values that are often contrary to God's covenant people. The Church and Home should not only be places where virtue is determined but cultivated, and this means parents should not give up and take the easy way out, and it means children should not be obstinate and disregard their parent's instruction.

3. Lastly, we should be diligent to take our cues from Scripture and not the world. Children are not a burden or an obstacle to living our lives as we please or being our authentic selves – quite the contrary, children are incredible blessings in that they show us a depth of intimacy we never knew existed. They provide a real-life analogy of God's great love and patience for us as His children. They provide a path and agency of God's great plan of redemption as He uses their lives for His Kingdom. They provide a window into many great theological and practical truths, and should never be discarded as unnecessary or outside of God's will for our life.

A similar caution is proper on the other side of this pendulum – children should not become so important that our self-worth hinges upon them. The inability to have kids doesn't render you incapable of serving and enjoying God. If you do have children, the status of them should not be pursued because of what sort of status it may bring to you. Children are a great blessing, but they can easily become idols for those who don't have them and want them, or simply objects for those who do have them but use them.

Scripture teaches that children belong to one's family, but in God's covenant people, they are first and foremost *His*. This belonging to God means our diligence to raise them, care for them, or even be a good child to our parents is directly correlated with how we care for anything that belongs to God. We help raise them under the Lordship of Christ not because we want society to think better of them or ourselves but because we recognize that doing so will lead to God's glory and their joy, and therefore our joy as well. And, of course, just like everything else that is good, it will, in fact, be a blessing to the world.

1 What was your childhood like? Strict? Lenient? Legalistic? Irreligious? How did this impact you?

2 What are three things you wish you had heard more as a child or that you would want to tell your children?

3 Pray that God would help children of the next generation be discipled and raised with love and honor.

FATHER

DAY TWO

As you read, write down your observations and ask, *what is the purpose?*

I had a good father growing up. He was patient, kind, wise, humble – always looking to serve. Don't get me wrong, he was imperfect, but he knew that, and it made him lean on God. I never questioned whether he loved me, which is why I was surprised at how meaningful it was when I received a letter from him that I didn't expect.

We were at an event where many men were getting letters from their fathers. I looked around and saw how impactful these letters were, especially for those who had a strained relationship with their father. I thought that was really wonderful and was thanking God that he had blessed me with a good father when all of a sudden an envelope was offered to me from mine.

I don't know how they got ahold of him, but it caught me off guard. I didn't think I needed it. I knew my father loved me; I always had. But I opened this unexpected letter and began to read my father's words for me. It overtook me. I discovered something; whether you have a broken or healthy father, there are few things that rival the feeling you get when you hear his love for you.

The image of 'father' is one God utilizes often. It echoes in the very beginning of Genesis when God creates Adam and Eve, 'in His image.' They bear the mark of their creator like a father to a child, not because they look like Him physically (God is not physical), but because they seem like Him. They care and cultivate; they reproduce life; they share His rule and reign. In fact, every covenant has a 'father' figure who informs the collective.

Adam was a father figure for the whole world (Lk. 1, Rom. 5, 1 Cor. 15). Noah, too, served this purpose as humanity restarts. Abraham became the father of many nations (we know the song). In our New Covenant, Jesus explains that we are to speak to our Father (Mt. 6:9), that Jesus was the Son sent from the Father (Jn. 3:16), and that the only way to the Father is through Jesus (Jn. 14). This is important to understand – you only call God "Father" through Jesus by the Holy Spirit, and you belong to Jesus in covenant relationship.

The weight of this father/son relationship is elaborated in Romans 7-8 as Paul contrasts the old covenant with the new. He talks about both the beauty and the problems within the old covenant, but now that the new has arrived, there is an adoption for all those who would be found in Christ. We are given a Spirit of adoption, which shows us to be children of God. God is our Father – and he has written a 'Word,' a letter of love that transcends cultural alphabets, a word which becomes visible by incarnating into our present reality for eyes to behold. The Jesus of history becomes the expression of God's love and the exact representation of His being (Heb. 1).

Now it's time to reflect on an important theological point that informs every other part of how we understand our lives. Every relationship, every activity, every blessing is meant to give us a glimpse into our life with God. There is a reciprocal relationship between how God informs what is good and how our experience of what is good informs our understanding of God. I'm going to call this – **Theological Transference.**

Let me give you an example: Let's say I have to go away on deployment when my son is too young to remember me. Years pass and while gone, I create a Lego set for him that, once built, will be a full-sized mechanical replica of me (This is terrifying I know, but it's an analogy so just come with me).

My son takes and builds this replica, and when it is finally complete, he stands there in awe and excitement. He did not know my face, but now he knows how tall I am, what I look like, how incredibly muscular I am, etc. Now, there is something good here to be enjoyed by my son, and when it is built correctly, it allows him to see the best way it operates, it allows him to look back at its creator and have affection and awe for him; Trusting not only that his father really loves him (I came up with the gift, I created the gift, I made sure all the pieces would be correct, and then I gave it to him to enjoy), but also enjoying something truly wonderful that was made for him.

But there is more – it also tells him something about his father in particular. The ability to follow directions exactly doesn't just mean he has a life-size toy but that he actually has an understanding of what his father looks like.

Now let's say that he lost some pieces. In fact, they were crucial. He lost the mechanism that made the replica move, and he didn't follow the directions as he put it together, so not only does it not move, it looks nothing like me at all. It looks like a Picasso painting or some scary monster. He believes he has finished its construction, and he is disappointed. It looks nothing like what he thought, it doesn't move, and now he has extra pieces he has no idea what to do with.

Perhaps he blames the instructions, perhaps he blames himself, perhaps he blames me, but he won't see me anymore. He will get caught up in his own wounds or think I did this as a trick. Hopefully, you understand the point I'm trying to make.

DAY TWO

God as Father not only means he gives us good gifts to enjoy, but that he gives us these things as a way of communicating Himself – but what if we mess them up? Not only will we not enjoy the gift, but our inability to see what He intended it to be will actually change how we see the Giver! And this becomes even more emphasized by earthly fathers, who generally possess some level of imperfection and brokenness.

You see, God gives the gift of fatherhood not so that men can have some human to take care of for a while but because in this blessing, its purpose and function actually point back to God. Fatherhood communicates something to us about who God is. We see God clearer by being a father or having one.

But what if we mess it up? What if we broke something? Lost something? **Perhaps we will blame the instructions, perhaps blame ourselves, perhaps we will blame the Giver, but we also won't understand God.** Instead, we will perpetuate a brokenness that moves away from seeing God and perhaps become an obstacle to what it truly means to want a Father at all.

Yet, in God's covenant with His people, He is Father. Therefore fathers must, as His covenant people, be good fathers, not only so that they can enjoy the gift of fatherhood in all the ways it was intended, but because they can point others toward who God is as Father.

This **Theological Transference** informs every relationship, activity, and blessing – as a child, father, mother, wife, husband, painter, engineer, and every other good thing on this earth. God infuses it with purpose and joy to point back toward Himself as the person of purpose and joy.

1 How would you define the idea 'Theological Transference,' and what difference does it make?

2 What sorts of characteristics does Scripture ascribe to being a Father? In what ways did you see these in your father or your own fatherhood?

3 Pray that God would give you healthy ways to understand fatherhood that restore what you may have known or affirm what you've enjoyed.

COVENANT HOME

MOTHER

DAY THREE

As you read, write down your observations and ask, *what is the purpose?*

If Scripture gives wisdom toward being a child and father, then, of course, it provides wisdom toward being a mother. In many ways, this wisdom is paired with parental guidance like, "*start children off on the way they should go, and even when they are old they will not depart from it*" (Prov. 22:6), but it gets more specific as well, attributing maternal characteristics to God as He cares for Israel, of Israel as it cares for the covenant persons, and simply for mothers as they pass on their covenant faithfulness to the next generation.

Mothers possess a nurturing quality that is unrivaled. Growing up, when I wanted to play, I wanted Dad, but when I was sick or hurting, I wanted Mom. The nurturing characteristics of a mother are the most prominent throughout Scripture and probably the most fundamental to motherhood. A unique bond and intimacy is formed in the womb, which only grows deeper and deeper.

I'm sure many of us think of that famous book, *Love You Forever*, where a mother raises her son, each night bringing him to bed and singing the promise of her love. What you may not know is that the book was written by the children's author Robert Munsch. He wrote the book after he and his wife birthed two stillborn babies. He said that the song came to him as a testament to how he and his wife felt about their lost children, a love that transcended space, time, and life itself.

The book ends with the mother unable to go to him, to lift him, to sing, so instead, the son comes to his ailing mother, no doubt nearing the end of her life, lifts her, and sings that lullaby over her. The nurturing love which poured out from her own heart was what raised him into the man that he was, and it rebounded toward the same love which he used to lift her and entangle them forever, beyond space, time, and life itself.

When we see the characteristics of true motherhood throughout Scripture, it has these qualities. God is described as taking Israel under His wings as a mother eagle (Dt. 32:11-12; Mt. 23:37-38), as producing Israel out of His own womb and comforting them (Dt. 32:18, Is. 66:13), as Israel nursing the people toward covenant faithfulness (Is. 66:11), even as Paul speaks of his own ministry (1 Thess. 2:7) as well as his affirmation of the role women played in who Timothy became (2 Tim. 1:3-5).

It appears that the greatest role of a mother is to nurture their child to become all that God intends, which is first and foremost, a covenant person. God's covenant person. If parents raise their children to be athletes, engineers, artists, or counselors; if they become mothers or fathers or neighbors or friends, but they do not belong to the covenant people, the child has recieved only a portion of what they were made for.

Notice in Galatians that Paul identifies two covenant women, Hagar and Sarah. If you'd like to read that story, you can return to Genesis 12-23, but Paul explains the theological significance. There is one mother who is the result of trying to take our lives into our own hands. Abraham knew God was going to bless him, but he didn't wait on God. He took Hagar and tried to force blessing through his own achievements. Sarah, on the other hand, was God's promise. The Covenant of Grace came through her, not because of anything Abraham or Sarah had done or would do but through God's gracious love.

Paul is essentially asking the Galatians which mother they belong to because our mothers matter. They form us. They nurture us. They shape us. Do you belong to a mother of promise or performance? That's the question. And the wisdom we receive when we consolidate all of this data is that belonging to the right covenant mother paves the way for belonging to the right covenant God.

REFLECTION

1 What important roles do mothers play, and how well did you receive or embody those characteristics?

2 In what ways do you nurture your children, or others, toward faith in Christ and His covenant people?

3 Pray to God for godly mothers. Maybe it is your mother, you as a mother, your wife as a mother, or just healthy mothers to help God's covenant people thrive.

GOING
DEEPER

GOD'S GENDER

We speak of God as Father, and Scripture also describes God with maternal characteristics, so does God have a gender? The quick answer is no. Gender is tied to biological sex and God has no body, but man and woman are endowed with qualities which point us back to the attributes of God, therefore how we speak of God's pronouns matter and the article below is a helpful summary of why.

SMALL GROUP
ROUND TABLE

SMALL TALK

What is your earliest childhood memory?

GOOD TALK

What stuck out this week in the study?

What questions or thoughts did you have as you read?

REAL TALK

What sorts of things have you 'theologically transferred' from your father or mother to God?

DO SOMETHING DIFFERENT

Our homes are environments that shape us more than any other, for good and for bad. We can become resentful towards the decisions our parents have made, or we can be blessed by those decisions, but we are always called by God to reflect upon them. Often what parents feel were shortcomings in their childhood rebound into reactionary parenting, which is more concerned with "not
parenting like that" instead of parenting like God.

Work with a loved one to develop specific values in your life (church, friends, family, sports, school), list them out in how you spend time with them currently, and add the activities which go along with them. How can you cultivate a household that prioritizes God's presence in each area and its level of importance? What priorities need to change? Take time and pray for wisdom to discern how to prioritize rightly and make changes that will last.

PRAYER REQUESTS

WEEK FOUR

COVENANT MARRIAGE

EPHESIANS 5:22-23

Wives, submit yourselves to your own husbands as you do to the Lord. For the husband is the head of the wife as Christ is the head of the church, his body, of which he is the Savior. Now as the church submits to Christ, so also wives should submit to their husbands in everything.

Husbands, love your wives, just as Christ loved the church and gave Himself up for her to make her holy, cleansing her by the washing with water through the word, and to present her to Himself as a radiant church, without stain or wrinkle or any other blemish, but holy and blameless. In this same way, husbands ought to love their wives as their own bodies. He who loves his wife loves himself. After all, no one ever hated their own body, but they feed and care for their body, just as Christ does the church— for we are members of His body. "For this reason a man will leave his father and mother and be united to his wife, and the two will become one flesh." This is a profound mystery—but I am talking about Christ and the church. However, each one of you also must love his wife as he loves himself, and the wife must respect her husband.

SEPTEMBER 28 / OCTOBER 1, 2023

SERMON NOTES

Catch up or rewatch the sermon
from this week at cco.church/sermons

COVENANT MARRIAGE

COVENANT MARRIAGE

LOVE

DAY ONE

As you read, write down your observations and ask, *what is the purpose?*

The growing statistics of divorce and trends of sexual promiscuity indicate that we do not understand marriage. We do not understand sex. If *theological transference* means anything, it is especially relevant to this topic, where the breakdown of physical and spiritual union results in painful ruin. It is hard to imagine anything more destructive than the failure of a marriage. I don't mean to open new wounds for anyone who has been a victim or perpetrator of these failures, and I don't mean to exclude those who are single from this guide as we explore the concept of marriage. In fact, I want to state outright that my main concern here is less about how to improve one's marriage (although this is a concern) and instead about how marriage tells us something about God. Ephesians 5 unpacks exactly what that is.

Ephesians 5 starts by unpacking the dual concepts of submission and love. Submission and love are the two ingredients that make a marriage soar. Many in our cultural moment balk at the suggestion that women should submit to their husbands; the irony is that many in the original historical context would have balked at the demand for men to love their wives. The Bible is less concerned about appeasing the changing demands of culture and, instead, seeks to provide a consistent truth that will lead to God's glory and our joy.

Many who study this passage focus so significantly on the concepts of submission and love as they relate to the practical outworking of a marriage that they fail to see Paul's central point: Marriage is perhaps the most meaningful analogy toward how we understand our relationship with God. Every demand marriage places on us is not arbitrary; it is bound up in the Maker's design to teach us something about who He is and who we are.

You can see it throughout the text. Ephesians talks about women submitting to their husbands and husbands loving their wives. The role of a husband is to do everything possible, even at the cost to himself, to present his wife to God as holy and beautiful. He is called to feed and care for his wife as if it were his own body.

Ephesians then recalls the story of Adam and Eve, the first two individuals created in God's image who, in their union, display the divine program. The "two will become one flesh," but what does Ephesians say? This two-to-one has less to do with the beauty of union in marriage than it does with the blessing of union with Christ! The reason submission and love become two meaningful ingredients to a healthy marriage is that they are the same meaningful ingredients to a healthy relationship with Christ!

The analogy of marriage with Christ may sound strange, but it wouldn't to many Jews. In fact, the New Covenant in Christ was the restoration of a failed marriage.

The accusation of infidelity was one of the chief complaints of the Old Testament prophets. Over and over again, the prophets saw the willingness to forsake covenant with God comparable to a sexual affair. In fact, the book of Hosea uses the prophet Hosea's life as one big analogy of human unfaithfulness. God calls Hosea to marry a prostitute who continually puts herself back on the market despite Hosea's great care for her, and his willingness to buy her back.

It must be said once more – I don't intend to reopen wounds or bang on someone's guilt; quite the contrary. If our New Covenant relationship with Christ tells us anything, it is that anything can be redeemed! This redemption is Ephesians' point from the very beginning. You were dead in your trespasses, separate from a life with God, yet Christ came roaring back, fighting for a bride at the cost of His own life. Ephesians says, *"Christ loved the church and gave Himself up for her to make her holy, cleansing her by the washing with water through the word, and to present her to Himself as a radiant church, without stain or wrinkle or any other blemish, but holy and blameless."* (Eph. 5:25-27).

Marriage is God's great gift, not just for a husband and wife to enjoy, but to point back to the same sort of union He is inviting us to in Christ. But *theological transference* reminds us that, while marriage is first and foremost about God, it must also be informed by God. Wives must submit to their husbands, and husbands must love their wives, and in this way, we begin to enjoy marriage in its utmost, but also have a model for what it means to enjoy God in His utmost. To misunderstand marriage in this way is to misunderstand our relationship with Christ, where He loves and we submit. It is in light of Christ's love that we are motivated to submit.

And this, too, informs our marital exchange: Husbands are called to sacrifice themselves for the good and holiness of their wives. The only reason a wife would not want to submit to her husband is because she doesn't actually believe he would die for her – and she very well may be right!

DAY ONE

Submission and love can become challenging to exchange in a fallen world where one spouse has compromised their divine calling. There is no doubt that Paul understands this as he pens the letter, which is why Paul's call to men is to love, not because their wife submits, but because they were loved by Christ and must submit to Him. Paul's call to women is to submit to their husbands, not because their husband perfectly loves, but because they have been perfectly loved by Christ. It is our union in Christ, our belonging to God, that we fulfill His calling.

And perhaps it will be in this submission and love that God uses a person to change their spouse toward godliness and subvert the powers of sin and death – this is undoubtedly what happens in Christ's own submission and love, as He gave himself over to death and emerged victorious in resurrection (1 Pet. 3).

1 What is the purpose of marriage, and what implications does that have for our relationship with God?

2 Do you have any friends that are a part of God's covenant people but are currently struggling in their marriage?
In what ways can you be an encouragement to them?

3 Pray that God would help our marriages be healthy testimonies of who God is and what He has called us to be.

COVENANT MARRIAGE

PURITY

DAY TWO

As you read, write down your observations and ask, *what is the purpose?*

Purity and holiness are often mentioned together but are sometimes difficult to understand. Holiness tends to speak of something set apart, and purity tends to identify the condition of something which makes it worthwhile to be set apart. The best analogy I've heard is in the concept of a toothbrush.

A toothbrush is "holy" in that it is set apart for a specific purpose. My toothbrush has been set apart to clean my teeth, which means it isn't going anywhere else. I'm not going to use it to clean the toilets, the floors, my shoes; I'm not going to use it to eat with or play drums; it has one purpose that it must be set apart for—my teeth. And the toothbrush must be kept pure for this purpose. If the toothbrush drops in the sink, on the floor—God forbid, in the toilet—it must be purified. If it can't be purified, it must be thrown out.

When we speak about marriage being pure, it has many of these same connotations—every covenant does. It is important to recognize that marriage is a covenant as we talk about how to live in covenant relationship with God and His people. A covenant is 'holy' in that it sets apart a relationship from all others. This holiness is especially true when it is with a God who is, in essence, holy and when we receive specific relationships He gives us, like marriage.

The purity of any covenant has to do with how well the conditions and promises of that covenant are upheld. If they are broken or trespassed, the relationship itself is no longer 'holy' or set apart from all others. A covenant becomes impure when we've let foreign concepts, behaviors, and/or individuals into an agreement they don't belong in or when we have left the agreement because we've entered a new one with others.

Now, God has defined the marriage covenant for us. Marriage isn't just a legal institution; it is especially Christian. It's crucial we understand this because marriage is so engrained into the Western mindset that it is hard to imagine any other way, but if we ask where marriage came from, there is only one answer – God. A quick skim through history will make this very evident.

Men and women have always had sexual relationships, but it has not always been marriage. Marriage, in particular, is defined by God as an exclusive (two people), complementary (man/woman), practically useful, intimate, lifelong union *under God* (Gen. 2:18, 23-24; 3:16; Eph. 5:25; Rom. 7; Heb. 13:4; Deut. 17:17). Anything else is not a marriage. It may be a sexual partnership, it may be social convenience, but it is not marriage.

The idea of purity is especially potent because it contains within it what sort of condition a marriage is in by maintaining these qualities; to maintain exclusivity, complementarity, practical benefit, and lifelong intimacy under God is to have a pure marriage, but along the way, there can be breakdown.

Now, just because there is some breakdown doesn't mean the marriage must be discarded any more than dropping the toothbrush in the sink means it can't be used for its purpose. The toothbrush can be cleaned and utilized again; it can be redeemed, so too can marriage.

Perhaps the greatest threat to the purity of a marriage is our appetite for pleasure. Western culture has adopted an individualistic attitude toward sexual pleasure that has made it more like eating fast food than climbing a mountain. Instead of beauty, we have buffet. Here, you can pick and choose what you have and when you want it.

There is a strange myth of Christianity regarding sex: Christians are private prudes who hate physical joy. It is a strange myth considering we have an entire book in our Bible that celebrates the wonder of physical intimacy. In fact, the Christian view of sex is not that we think little of it, but we think so highly of it. It is not just fun and games but beauty and wonder. It isn't just skin but intimacy. It isn't about what we can get out of someone, but what we can give to someone. To guard this sacred joy for marriage isn't to become stuffy or prudish about sex, but to lift it toward its glorious purpose, where two lives become one and deep vulnerability is exchanged and enjoyed. It is mystery, and it is good.

What we must understand about maintaining purity in our marriage is not just that it is protecting the family, the relationship, our mutual trust, and joy, but that it sings of a higher truth that finds its expression in God himself. Every covenant has boundaries, and our ability to respect those boundaries is meant to provide more freedom and joy, not less.

I'm not sure I know anyone who has compromised their covenant marriage and found greater joy on the other side – and God is inviting us to use the purity of our marriage to have and to hold, but also so that we recognize that no law is made for our burden but for our joy. Marriage is once more a foreground for what God blesses us with and invites us to as we enjoy covenant relationship with Him.

One last note about the redemption of marriage that becomes extremely pivotal as to why this topic is necessary for every person: You may be asking, at what point does a marriage become so impure that it becomes irredeemable? I'm sure we all know people we love that have been in difficult circumstances which can be hard to navigate. However, the answer to this question is the same regarding people who have broken their covenant relationship with God!

Scripture teaches that when both believers belong to God and His covenant people, *anything can be redeemed.* When you belong to a resurrecting God, there is nothing too dead for Him – our lives are living testimonies of that reality. The purity of marriage doesn't just help us understand what type of relationship God has called us to embody but what sort of healing God provides when we fail.

1 Explain what concepts God infuses marriage with.
How do those concepts speak to our covenant relationship with God?

2 What concepts does culture advocate about marriage?
Have any of those concepts crept into what you expect of God in your
covenant relationship with Him?

3 Pray that God would help you overcome the temptations which
compromise your purity.

COVENANT MARRIAGE

UNION

DAY THREE

*READ THROUGH 1 CORINTHIANS 6:7-20 +
MALACHI 2:13-16.*

As you read, write down your observations and ask, *what is the purpose?*

Often in a marriage ceremony, there is some demonstration of unity. It could be sand mixed into a single vase, a knot tied with two pieces of rope, or perhaps even a puzzle that is assembled, but the most popular symbol of unity in our culture is the unity candle.

Typically, the unity candle gesture will include two slim white candles that possess their own flame. During the ceremony, they stand behind each person as a symbolic representation, but once the vows and rings are exchanged, each person grabs their candle and together fuse their flames to make a new bigger flame on one bigger candle, and blow out their original flame, indicating that they have been unified. They are 'one flesh.' They are not who they once were; they are no longer just a man or just a woman, but husband and wife – their lives now intertwined.

This unified reality is borne out in every part of their life, extending even to their name, as the woman's last name (typically) is changed to the man's. They don't lose their first name or their individuality, but they share a last name and a unity. They are no longer just themselves, but neither are they erased – they are one and many.

Now, the book of Corinthians is all about unity. Paul writes to a church that has significant issues that are causing division. His answer to this division is love, which is beautifully elaborated upon in 1 Corinthians 13, that chapter which is often used in weddings. It is love that overcomes division and provides a way for self-giving and unity, but in our current passage, Paul is explicitly dealing with the role of sex.

Without going into too much explanation, there was sexual immorality in the church, compromising the unity within families and the unity within the church. Paul is specifically addressing the false idea that our bodies don't make a difference since they are headed for a grave. He says they make a difference because they are intrinsically a part of us. We are a unity of body and soul. When the resurrection comes, we won't just be a strange spirit, and we also won't just be reincarnated into some random body; we will be both body and soul. Body and soul are tied together in a unity, which means what happens to your body is also connected to what's happening to your soul, and vice versa.

Paul says this is especially important to understand because you have joined into a unity with Christ. If you share a unity with Christ – why would you sow division in your own body by joining in a union with someone or something else? He specifically points to sex with a prostitute as an example of this distorted unity, insinuating that sex itself acts as a sort of unifying event which ties one body to another and makes them, 'one flesh.'

This example is supposed to give rise to another thought: just as you can be united in body with another person, God unites with us in spirit. Paul actually goes on to say that the husband's body no longer belongs to himself but to his wife, and vice versa. The individuals are not erased, but they now share life, and Paul's point is to say that this is true of our relationship with God as well. Again, marriage, just like all good gifts, has *theological transference*, which means that it is both ours to enjoy and also God's to define. In doing so, we know God and ourselves.

Paul is saying that we should not engage in immorality because it compromises our unity with God. Just like sex with a prostitute would compromise your unity with your spouse, engaging in immorality compromises your relationship with God. You are one with Him. You belong to Him. The more our marriages reflects these realities, the more our covenant relationship with God will reflect these realities.

Paul knows this, and he knows it impacts the covenant people as well. Paul is saying that we should maintain the integrity of our unity by ripping out that which hinders it and leaning into that which vitalizes it. Love, the willing of another's good, will be the force that brings us to unity.

However, this also means that divorce is, in essence, contrary to what God wills for marriage. Divorce shatters covenant relationship. Our culture has made marriage into a consumer product. It is contractual. It supports an attitude of "you scratch my back, I scratch yours, but as soon as you aren't upholding your end of the deal, I can leave." Sometimes marriage doesn't even maintain that level of contract but simply becomes about the satisfaction of the self in particular.

Our culture says that marriage is about self-fulfillment, not self-giving, and in doing so, our culture lays the groundwork for marriages to be abandoned and unity destroyed at the drop of a hat; a destruction that echoes past the two individuals and into the lives of their kids, extended families, and communities.

God's covenant people are meant to be defined differently. They are called to be self-giving, self-sacrificial, committed, and pure, not only because this godliness leads to flourishing but because it teaches us about who God is and who we are. It affirms our security in Christ and His unyielding covenant love, which is not based on performance, but grace. So long as divorce, or any other sort of disunity, proliferates among God's people, we will find ourselves questioning God's covenant love, and others will too; we will turn into legalists who think it must be earned each day, or we will turn into rebels who don't believe it can be repaired.

Yet covenants transcend contracts. Covenants are lifelong and are intended to provide relational security. The strength of a covenant is as strong as the persons who made it; their faithfulness, their goodness, their grace. What we see in our covenant with God is a total dependence on Him. What God attempts to demonstrate in Christ is not only that we will never have to fear or mistrust God's faithfulness but that His forever-enduring love can breathe life back into us.

REFLECTION

1 Why is unity such an important characteristic for our relationships?

2 What sorts of activities threaten unity or support it?
Do you see any of these activities in your own life?

3 Pray that God would continue to unify marriages and the Church as we share fellowship under the name of Christ.

GOING
DEEPER

THE PURPOSE OF SEX/GENDER

In a world that is increasingly blurring the definitions of male and female, the Bible gives more precision and objectivity. In summary, males exist, and females exist, and they are not confused. There are fundamental differences that go beyond mere biological parts and include interdependent design so that each gender complements the other. God has called, and gifted men and women for good works and unique offices, and this short article begins to explain how those things manifest themselves in God's church and the world.

SMALL TALK

What do you catch yourself doing that has made you think, "Oh my gosh, I am my mom/dad?"

GOOD TALK

What stuck out this week in the study?

What questions or thoughts did you have as you read?

REAL TALK

Marriage can be a sensitive topic because we all have different backgrounds of family history, spiritual maturity, biblical literacy, and religious background – how has this week challenged you, or what questions does it leave you with?

Are you taking your cues for Biblical marriage from culture or covenant?

(If you are the leader, write the questions down and think over them during the week. Don't try to answer them immediately. In fact, encourage the one who asked the question to seek wisdom from Scripture, and both of you compare notes the next week.)

DO SOMETHING DIFFERENT

As we have said before, so goes the family, so goes the society. We, as the Church, have a commitment to live our lives in a way that honors and reflects God and our covenant relationship with Him. The purpose of this week is not to leave anyone feeling the burden of guilt but the motivation to love and serve the faithful God who offers us forgiveness and healing when we fail. God provides an ethic that is meant to be a blessing to our lives and be flourishing for our community, so consider how you might live faithfully in your own marriage or how you can be a support for someone who is struggling with theirs.

PRAYER REQUESTS + QUESTIONS

WEEK FIVE

COVENANT CITIZENSHIP

2 CORINTHIANS 5:16-21

So from now on we regard no one from a worldly point of view. Though we once regarded Christ in this way, we do so no longer. Therefore, if anyone is in Christ, the new creation has come: The old has gone, the new is here! All this is from God, who reconciled us to Himself through Christ and gave us the ministry of reconciliation: that God was reconciling the world to Himself in Christ, not counting people's sins against them. And He has committed to us the message of reconciliation. We are therefore Christ's ambassadors, as though God were making His appeal through us. We implore you on Christ's behalf: Be reconciled to God. God made Him who had no sin to be sin for us, so that in Him we might become the righteousness of God.

OCTOBER 5 / OCTOBER 8, 2023

SERMON NOTES

Catch up or rewatch the sermon
from this week at cco.church/sermons

COVENANT CITIZENSHIP

COVENANT CITIZENSHIP

KINGDOM

DAY ONE

As you read, write down your observations and ask, *what is the purpose?*

We all love a disruptive question: "Is a hot dog a sandwich?" "Does the toilet paper go over or under the holder?" "Does pineapple belong on pizza?" "How is 'GIF' pronounced?" There is no shortage of disruptive questions. However, some questions are so disruptive that we try to never ask them, like, "Are you Republican or Democrat?" "Are you for vaccines or against them?" "What sins do you have to confess?"– Now, *these* are disruptive questions. The reason is because they are starting to hit closer to home. Instead of a quibble over a useless opinion, we have competing beliefs that are rooted in our values. We are starting to hit closer to our identities.

Here in our text we see Pilate ask a disruptive question, "Are you the King of the Jews?" This question is disruptive for many reasons: 1. The guys delivering Jesus over to Pilate are Jews, so for Jesus to answer affirmatively would appear to be a contradiction to His claim. 2. The guy questioning Jesus has allegiance to the King of Rome, a Caesar who demands that all opposing kings kneel or die. 3. A "no" answer might let Jesus off the hook, but it would compromise His identity and mission. So, what does Jesus say? "My kingdom is not of this world."

Jesus masters disruptive questions, not just because He is able to answer the question with precision and truth, but because He is able to shift the question to its true essence – Pilate wants to know if Jesus is a king, and Jesus affirms that He is, but not one that is of this world. For Pilate, the threat becomes neutralized. He thinks Jesus is innocent and should be set free, but he gives the Jewish people an option – do you want Jesus or Barabbas? A delusional "king" or a murderous revolutionary? They pick the latter and, by doing so, clarify that their covenant relationship has gone all wrong.

We actually see this all throughout the Gospels. Jesus is constantly getting into disputes about the old covenants and their expectations and laws. The way Jews sabbath, take oaths, judge, pray, and affiliate with outsiders was indicative of the old covenants, but Jesus came to fulfill and redefine those principles, and it ruffled some feathers. This new teaching Jesus brings is most clearly seen in the Sermon on the Mount in Matthew 5-7.

The hostility Jesus is involved in is why He is placed on trial. He is subverting the ways, not just of the old covenant, but of the world, and you must choose which king you will serve. When you enter into covenant relationship with God, it must be done with Jesus as King. You are a citizen of a heavenly country, a chosen race, a royal priesthood (1 Pet. 2:9-10).

In God's covenant community, your allegiance is first and foremost to your God, not your country, your family, your sports teams, or your job. You belong to a Kingdom which may not be of this earth, but it is subverting and subduing it until the consummation of eternity breaks out upon it (Dan. 2). You must pick the kingdom of light or darkness. The kingdom of God or the world, the way of Jesus or Barabbas. Barabbas walked away happy but would die; Jesus walked into death but would live forever.

1. What does it mean for the Kingdom of God to not be of this world?

2. How does your heavenly citizenship show up in your earthly citizenship? What is different about how you engage your country? Family? Sports teams? Job?

3. Pray the Lord's prayer today: *"Our Father in heaven, hallowed be your name, your kingdom come, your will be done, on earth as it is in heaven. Give us today our daily bread. And forgive us our debts, as we also have forgiven our debtors. And lead us not into temptation, but deliver us from the evil one."* (Mt. 6:9-13)

CULTURE

*READ THROUGH MATTHEW 28:16-20 +
GENESIS 1:26-31.*

As you read, write down your observations and ask, *what is the purpose?*

A covenant with God puts His people at the center of God's plan across space and time. Quite contrary to the claims of modern science and psychology, we are not specks of dust randomly floating around in a universe that cares nothing for us, but the image bearers of a God who is actively at work in and through us. We see this at the beginning of Genesis when God creates Adam and Eve. Here we see two image bearers coming together to cultivate the earth toward being a dwelling place for God and Man. The very waters of Eden pour down from its dwelling to invade the earth and bring life into it (Gen. 2:8-14). In this initial covenant with Adam and Eve, we see the very center of God's activity, personality, and will, and the covenant is the vehicle by which God's presence overflows into the world.

When God makes a covenant with people, they become the location of His activity. In many ways, this means that every moment of history begins and ends in light of the covenant God and His people. Everything is ordered around God and His plan. Every world power is being built and utilized, not for its glory, but God's. The ebb and flow of the universe is directly tied to God and His people.

From Adam to Noah, to Abraham, to Moses/Israel, to David – God embeds particular promises to have universal ramifications. The reason prophets, judges, and kings can speak about the future of God's dealings is because God is specifically ordering the world toward its perfect culmination in Christ. Christ is the new Adam who takes on the cultural mandate to grow and rule; the new Noah by which a family would be saved; the new Abraham by whom a nation would be born; the new Moses, who would deliver and live a better law, and the new David, who would reign supreme. Christ is the epicenter of every movement, of which the Church becomes particularly important.

We've tried to make the point that Christ is the perfect covenant head because He is the truly perfect one. In mysteriously wonderful ways, our entrance into covenant with God is an entrance into union with Christ. Like a marriage, Christ as groom enters into life with Church as bride (Eph. 5; Rev. 21). Neither identity is erased by their union, but now their identity is shared. This unity means that we share in Christ's work and purpose. We become "ambassadors" of Christ's reconciling work (2 Cor. 5:20). The task of the first Adam to grow and subdue has been taken up in Christ and now, by extension, the Church.

The Church is the beginning of the new dwelling of God's people, the new temple (Eph. 2; 1 Pet. 2; 1 Cor. 12). It is the Church where the waters of Eden flow once more by the Word of God (Jn. 4:13-14). We join into the epicenter of all history as it reverberates into God's wonderful plan. We are the location of God's activity, personality, and will. The ebb and flow of the universe is directly tied to God and His people – the Church.

Therefore, we heed God's commissioning to us; we listen to His command; we receive the cultural mandate as our mission to the world: "*Go and make disciples of all nations, baptizing them in the name of the Father and of the Son and of the Holy Spirit, and teaching them to obey everything I have commanded you. And surely I am with you always, to the very end of the age.*" (Mt. 28:19-20).

We are the new dwelling, the temple, the garden whose boundaries are expanding to envelop the entire world.

This means that every part of our lives matter. We are not just subjects of culture but cultivators. We are not simply working for a paycheck, but a King. Our parenting is not just to create good citizens but godly ones. We belong to a heavenly country that is breaking out now. We pray, "Your kingdom come, your will be done," not as a distant fact of Christ's appearing, but a current inbreaking of eternity itself. A new conversion, a healed marriage, an answered prayer, all testify in part to what will be true in full – that resurrection has already begun.

1 What does it mean for Christ and the Church to be the epicenter of all historical events?

2 Do you currently live as a culture builder in God's kingdom? If so, how? If not, why?

3 Pray that the Church would not just be a receptacle of worldly culture but on the frontlines of creating a culture that blesses the world.

COVENANT CITIZENSHIP

CALLING

DAY THREE

READ THROUGH 1 CORINTHIANS 1:26-31.

As you read, write down your observations and ask, *what is the purpose?*

What am I to do with my life? How can I make my life meaningful? What purpose is there for me? These are good questions. They are questions that can keep us up late at night. Many of us ask these questions, and we put ourselves out there. We apply for an appealing position or maybe even hastily quit our jobs. Others of us ask these questions and then do nothing at all. We may quip, "God will open a door if He wants me to move," and use it as an excuse to remain idle and ineffectual. How do we gauge a calling? What does it mean to be called to something?

I want to answer these questions in a very practical way, but I can't begin there. Before we can answer what we are to do, we must first answer who we are to become. No profession, activity, or task will ever bring joy to your life if you skip the step of understanding who God has called you to be.

Here in 1 Corinthians, it wastes no time – you are first called to be *in Christ*. Before Christ, you were not 'wise,' you were not 'influential,' you were not 'of noble birth,' but God called you to be in Christ.

We could possibly be offended by what Paul is saying here. He is saying that when we did not belong to the covenant God, we had nothing to brag about. He is also saying that now, even in Christ, we have everything, but still no reason to brag. We possess nothing on our own that gives us a reason to boast! And this is the most important point to grasp when understanding your calling. **You were called to be in Christ not because of what you can give to God but because of what God is giving to you.**

If God wants to accomplish anything in your life, it is using your weakness to show His strength. Too many Christians want to build God's kingdom on earth yet have not given Him reign over their own hearts. Jesus asks us to pick up *our* cross and follow Him, but our calling first begins by being rescued by *His*; to believe that cross means life for us, even if we are facing death.

Our calling begins by coming to grips with our weaknesses and letting them become the stage for God's glory. This recognition happens first and foremost by getting our eyes on the King, on the cross, on the empty tomb. Jesus, who is our righteousness, holiness, and redemption, is our life. We are called to be in Him.

This demonstration of God's power in weakness has always been true of God's covenant people. How many barren women had kids that God used to keep His promises (Mt. 1)? How many armies must God overcome by marching (Josh. 6)? By sounds (Jdg. 7)? By stones (1 Sam. 17)? God is not interested in the most talented, the most successful, the most attractive. In fact, it is difficult for people like that to be interested in God.

God wants those who realize their best day is still pennies compared to the riches God is offering. God wants those who have need of a Savior. That's the call. Come and die. Give up those accomplishments. Abandon performance. There is a covenant relationship that will never fail, never disappoint, never compromise, and it is because it is not based on you at all.

This need of a Savior is where our calling begins; to behold and enjoy the King who demonstrates what it means to overcome strength through weakness. Only then can our lives be offered as useful to the Creator. It is only when we are more concerned with being *with* God that we will find joy in being made useful *for* God. Our calling is to belong to a covenant people, which is first and foremost *His*.

1 What is a nagging weakness in your life that you must give to God?

2 What does being 'in Christ' mean for your life?

3 Pray that your identity would not be in your performance but in the person of Christ. Pray that your joy and contentment would be found in what He has given, not what you give to Him.

GOING DEEPER

CHRISTIANS AND CULTURE

It can be challenging to know how to live in a world of so many shifting cultural values. Culture is often a mixed bag of blessing and curse, beauty and distortion, and it is up to the Christian to follow God's leading both in how they relate to culture and how they influence it. Below is a short article of some considerations to process as you consider both what God has called you from, and what God has called you to.

SMALL GROUP

ROUND TABLE

SMALL TALK

Is a hot dog a sandwich?

Does the toilet paper go over or under the holder?

Does pineapple belong on pizza?

How is *GIF* pronounced?

GOOD TALK

What stuck out this week in the study?

What questions or thoughts did you have as you read?

REAL TALK

What is an area of weakness that you have seen God work, or where you need to ask Him to work?

DO SOMETHING DIFFERENT

Our lives are often segmented into church and school, work and friendships, but this should not be the case. Belonging to the kingdom of God means His reign stretches over our entire lives, and belonging to His covenant means God has invited us into co-ruling with Him. We should see every part of our lives as contributing to building God's kingdom, and influencing our current culture.

What this does not mean is that we impose our earthly cultural background (American or otherwise) upon other unique cultural expressions, but that we promote a Biblical culture which makes use of the beauty, and disposes the distortion, each earthly culture contains. So how can you be a Biblical culture builder in your present dwelling space?

PRAYER REQUESTS

WEEK SIX

COVENANT COMMUNITY

GALATIANS 6:1-10

Brothers and sisters, if someone is caught in a sin, you who live by the Spirit should restore that person gently. But watch yourselves, or you also may be tempted. Carry each other's burdens, and in this way you will fulfill the law of Christ. If anyone thinks they are something when they are not, they deceive themselves. Each one should test their own actions. Then they can take pride in themselves alone, without comparing themselves to someone else, for each one should carry their own load. Nevertheless, the one who receives instruction in the word should share all good things with their instructor.

Do not be deceived: God cannot be mocked. A man reaps what he sows. Whoever sows to please their flesh, from the flesh will reap destruction; whoever sows to please the Spirit, from the Spirit will reap eternal life. Let us not become weary in doing good, for at the proper time we will reap a harvest if we do not give up. Therefore, as we have opportunity, let us do good to all people, especially to those who belong to the family of believers.

OCTOBER 12 / OCTOBER 15, 2023

SERMON NOTES

Catch up or rewatch the sermon
from this week at cco.church/sermons

COVENANT COMMUNITY

COVENANT COMMUNITY

ETHIC

DAY ONE

As you read, write down your observations and ask, *what is the purpose?*

The Gospel of Matthew wants you to see how Jesus fulfills every part of the covenant of Moses. In fact, Matthew wants you to see that Jesus is a better Moses. He opens his Gospel with the birth of a child who is the fulfillment of the covenants with Abraham and David (Mt. 1; Ex. 1-2) and who is immediately in danger because of the edict of a King who feels threatened (Mt. 2; Ex. 1). Jesus grows up and is baptized only to enter into the wilderness for 40 days and 40 nights (Mt. 3-4; Ex. 14-18), and makes His way atop a mountain, but instead of receiving the words from God on tablets, Jesus starts speaking them Himself (Mt. 5-7; Ex. 19-24).

Jesus states, *"Do not think that I have come to abolish the Law or the Prophets; I have not come to abolish them but to fulfill them. For truly I tell you, until heaven and earth disappear, not the smallest letter, not the least stroke of a pen, will by any means disappear from the Law until everything is accomplished."* (Mt. 5:17-18) I want to keep playing this song until you can't get it out of your head – God is a faithful covenant-keeping God that you never need to mistrust. Every promise He has ever made will come true, every word will display itself in act, and we see this in the person and work of Jesus. Jesus is the fulfillment of all the covenants.

In Matthew 5, Jesus preaches a sermon providing a new ethic in light of His fulfillment and the New Covenant. In reality, the ethic doesn't differ substantially from the 10 commandments given to Moses, but it penetrates deeper. Instead of just restraining murder, we must restrain hate; instead of just restraining marital fidelity, we must restrain our eyes. Our falsehoods should be avoided, not by qualifying our words, but by giving them so much integrity that 'yes' means yes and 'no' means no.

Jesus is not changing the demands of the law but refining them toward their intended goal. God was never just after behavior modification, but our very heart. Fear can drive us to obedience out of duty even when we actually do want to hate, lust, lie – but love will drive us to obedience out of delight because our desires change from hate, from lust, from lies, to love, joy, and truth.

The demands of this ethic are steep, but they are the demands of God's covenant people. Jesus unsettles us when He says, "*For I tell you that unless your righteousness surpasses that of the Pharisees and the teachers of the law, you will certainly not enter the kingdom of heaven.*" (Mt. 5:20) He demands that hate, lust, and deception be eradicated from our hearts, or God cannot dwell there. The economy of God's kingdom is run on love; everything else is passing away. We have an ethic that separates us from the way of the world. But how could anyone live up to this ethic? How can we truly be the "salt of the earth, the city on a hill?" Only through Jesus.

As we've said before, Jesus is not only the covenant-keeping God who is faithful to His people but the covenant-keeping Man who enjoys the reward. Jesus is the righteousness that surpasses the Pharisees and teachers of the law, and it is only in Him that we experience fellowship with God.

More than that, it is only in Christ that we receive the presence of God's Spirit and produce the sorts of righteousness we could never produce on our own. The demands of Jesus are the expectations of how His covenant people will live, and the presence of the Holy Spirit is how God will accomplish this reality.

1. Do you find that your attempts to be 'moral' are out of duty or delight?
   If duty – what is keeping them from delight?
   If delight, what helped move them from duty?

2. What stuck out from Matthew 5 that you can commit to memory as an encouragement?

3. Pray that God would continue forming you into the righteous life He requires.

WORSHIP

READ THROUGH ROMANS 12:1-2 + MATTHEW 6-7.

As you read, write down your observations and ask, *what is the purpose?*

You've probably heard the phrase, "everybody worships." And it is true, of course, but the meaning of the word 'worship' can get lost in translation. What do we mean by it? Do we mean everyone has a god they say nice things to? Do we mean that everyone puts value on something that drives their life? Is worship something that happens at one point in time, like singing a song, or is it something that happens all the time based on what we think is most important? I think we can answer all these questions with "yes."

I like to compare it to a marriage, where there are formal and informal ways of communicating our relational depth. Informally—My wife and I are always married. Every part of our lives is impacted by that covenant relationship. I am in communication about what's going on, when things need to happen, asking questions, getting advice, looking for help. My entire life revolves around the give and take of our present needs and responsibilities.

In addition, since our covenant is exclusive, I'm not doing that with anyone else in the same way. My covenant relationship means there are boundaries and expectations that only make sense within this specific relationship. I'm not chatting with other girls, keeping all my money back for myself, or ignoring her communication; I'm engaged; I'm living as if she is presently with me; I wear our relationship everywhere because I love her.

But then the time comes for us to share unique space together. Formally—there is a way that this relationship finds meaningful expression. Let's say I take her out to dinner. I've planned it out: There are candles, rose petals, her favorite meal, a song that plays in the background, and a poem that will make her laugh at my ridiculousness. Here something formal is happening where the life we lived at a distance now becomes concentrated and enjoyed. This sort of dynamic is an analogy of our worship of God.

The informal aspects are how we live in our covenant relationship with God every single day. We live in a way whereby His Lordship impacts every aspect of our lives. We are in communication about what's going on and asking for help as needs and responsibilities present themselves. And it's exclusive. We're not relying on anything else outside of Him. Our entire life revolves around Him, and we are living as if He is presently with us (which, in God's case, He is!). We are a covenant people in relationship with a covenant God, so nothing we are, or do, is not touched by His reign.

This is why Paul can say, "Offer your bodies as living sacrifices," and why Jesus speaks about the authenticity needed to engage in true worship. God isn't looking for handouts or 'check-ins' but a life that is reoriented toward total dependence on God.

It is this sort of worship that happens in God's covenant people. Everybody does worship. Everybody is living for something or valuing something which drives them.

Maybe it is family, maybe it is friends, maybe it is professional achievement or the next physical pleasure, but what uniquely separates the people of God from the world is that our driving motivation, our ultimate value, is the glory and joy of our God. We worship according to an eternal person who never disappoints instead of a passing fad that is highly fragile. We are a worshipping community.

Next, we will look at the formal component of God's covenant people – when they gather for a concentrated experience of God's presence and love.

1 What is your typical schedule, and how does God impact those areas? Is there room for that impact to grow? Why or why not?

2 Are there things you do for or with God that become mere mental exercise instead of offering Him your real presence (prayer, service, giving, etc.)?

3 Pray that God would be the driving motivation of every part of your life and offer Him some specific areas where that can be improved.

COVENANT COMMUNITY

PRIORITY

DAY THREE

As you read, write down your observations and ask, *what is the purpose?*

Okay, let's catch up on our last devotion – everybody worships. Our worship is both what we do every single day and a unique concentration of the exchange of ourselves. These are what we called the informal and formal aspects of worship. The informal aspect is that I live every day in my covenant relationship with God and His people. His Lordship impacts my every moment and earthly activity.

The formal aspect is the concentrated exchange of ourselves. It's not just living as Christ is Lord but being in His presence. Of course, I don't mean to say that God is not present everywhere. He is. But God becomes uniquely present in ways that bring life and wonder to us. Like when He walks in the garden with Adam, or goes through the covenant pieces for Abraham, or leads the people of Israel through the wilderness, or shows Himself, even in the smallest degree, to Israel and Moses on a mountain.

The point is that when God becomes visible to our eyes, it isn't because He is now somewhere He wasn't before but because we have entered into something where we were not before. Scripture speaks of this happening in the weekly gathering, our Sunday morning worship. In our gatherings, we join in with all of God's people beyond space and time to share a concentrated space with God's presence, where He shows up in significant ways.

But wait – why don't we see Him? We don't experience God by sight; that's coming later. We experience God through our other senses. We hear the message of the Gospel proclaimed in ways which Christ becomes present to us (Rom. 10:14,17; 1 Pet. 1:8, 18-25; Gal. 3:1); through the table, we share in Christ's body and blood (Mt. 26:26-28; 1 Cor. 10:1-5, 11:23-32); through the waters of baptism (Rom. 6:1-7), through the songs we sing (Col. 3:15-17), and most importantly, through the very gathering of God's people who make up God's temple, His dwelling place (Eph. 2; 1 Pet. 2; 1 Cor. 12; Col. 1; Jn. 2, 4).

This presence in the gathering is why Hebrews implores the believers to *"not give up meeting together, as some are in the habit of doing, but encouraging one another—and all the more as you see the Day approaching."* (Heb. 10:25) We, as God's covenant people, prioritize the weekly gathering, not only because it becomes meaningful space to be with God but because it is in gathering as believers that this temple forms and invites Him to dwell. *We must gather, we must worship, we must praise, not out of duty, but delight.*

There is no relationship with God outside of His covenant people, and the covenant people are defined by their shared life with their covenant God. Not participating in the gathering is like being married but never seeing your wife. You might be able to make that last for a bit, but it isn't enough to sustain a healthy relationship. We were called to gather together and enjoy the presence of God, not only because of what we receive from this time but, equally important, because of what we give.

We must prioritize this time. It must become central. We were not made for online reflection. We were not made for occasional participation. We were not made to vacation apart from the presence of God but to seek His people wherever we are and join in with the praises which pour forth from our lives. Our covenant gatherings are not just one more event in our week to schedule; they are the epicenter of where heaven and earth collide, where bride and groom meet, where we receive a foretaste of what will be true for eternity.

1 Why do we practice baptism, Jesus' table, generosity, singing, and expounding upon God's Word?
What does this formal worship accomplish?

2 Why is it important to prioritize the gathering, and how well do you prioritize it?

3 Pray that the gathering of the local church would truly be a place where the Holy Spirit works to bring revival to each person who belongs to God's covenant people and an invitation to those who do not.

GOING DEEPER

WORSHIP

Worship includes both the way we live our lives (informal) and gather as God's dwelling place (formal). That being said, what are ways we worship? What all does that include? Is there a way to increase our time with God so that our informal and formal modes of worship are enhanced? Christ's Church has created a discipleship infrastructure meant to give specific ways you can be with God and enjoy Him. Below, you will find a QR code which links you to a section of our website that provides guidance on how to engage, both informally and formally. This engagement could be through small groups, Bible study, prayer, or many other ways which God has invited us to enjoy. If you are unsure, we also have provided a short assessment that you can take that will give you a place to start in your fellowship with God.

SMALL GROUP
ROUND TABLE

SMALL TALK

Where is the worst place to take someone on a date?

GOOD TALK

What stuck out this week in the study?

What questions or thoughts did you have as you read?

REAL TALK

What is harder to do, prioritize God in the informal, or formal?

What can you do to enhance that aspect of your worship and fellowship with God?

Everybody worships. The saying is true. The question is, what do you worship? Tim Keller provides a helpful way to begin to discern that question. He suggests that we consider what we daydream about. What enters the mind when we have downtime? Another way to discern the object of our worship is through looking at how you spend your time – what does your schedule look like? We should all analyze this question of worship every so often so that we are aware of the competing values in our life and attempt to reassert God as primary. Worshipping the right thing will lead to right joy, and God invites us to partake of that joy today.

PRAYER REQUESTS

COVENANT RESOURCES

ROMANS 12:3-8

For by the grace given me I say to every one of you: Do not think of yourself more highly than you ought, but rather think of yourself with sober judgment, in accordance with the faith God has distributed to each of you. For just as each of us has one body with many members, and these members do not all have the same function, so in Christ we, though many, form one body, and each member belongs to all the others. We have different gifts, according to the grace given to each of us. If your gift is prophesying, then prophesy in accordance with your faith. If it is serving, then serve; if it is teaching, then teach; if it is to encourage, then give encouragement; if it is giving, then give generously; if it is to lead, do it diligently; if it is to show mercy, do it cheerfully.

OCTOBER 19 / OCTOBER 22, 2023

SERMON NOTES

Catch up or rewatch the sermon
from this week at cco.church/sermons

COVENANT RESOURCES

POSSESSIONS

DAY ONE

READ THROUGH EXODUS 35:20-29 + ACTS 2:42-47.

As you read, write down your observations and ask, *what is the purpose?*

Growing up, my family didn't have much. We were often cared for by God's community, time and again seeing God's covenant people in action. I remember one time in particular when God showed us His faithfulness. I was probably nine years old at the time, and our family was going through a rough time financially. Not only that, but our cars were breaking down left and right. I grew up in a Christian home, so I had often been taught to bring my cares before God and pray, so that's what I did. I told my mom and dad that I would pray for a new car for our family.

Each night before bed, I asked that God would provide a car for our family that was good and reliable. I prayed to God for lots of things as a kid, but I was disciplined with this request. Lo and behold, a week later, I came home and my mom was ecstatic; someone had gifted us a car. She couldn't believe it. Heck, I can't say I wasn't a bit surprised myself! But the most amazing thing happened that day, not that we got a car (although that was amazing) but that God had taught me I never needed to worry again. He was taking care of us.

However, that car didn't fall out of the sky. It didn't materialize out of nothing right in front of our house; it was given in generosity and sacrifice by someone who cared. They cared because they belonged to God's covenant people. They cared because they cared about God and His people. When you belong to God, you no longer care so much about your possessions. Why would you? They are just things that are passing away. When you have a relationship with an eternal God and His eternal people, why hold on to what can become glory to God and a blessing to His people?

Exodus and Acts show two sides of how we can utilize our things for others, especially those who belong to God's family but don't have much. Exodus says that regardless of your material wealth, you can give to God for His glory. You can provide for the architecture of God's dwelling place. You can give up the values of earth because you've received the riches of heaven. The offerings people made went to build the tabernacle, the artifacts for worship, and to clothe and bless the priests who would serve them. We see here a demonstration of a generously sacrificial people for God's glory; that is who we are supposed to be.

In addition, Acts shows the Church as the new temple when the Spirit took up residence, not in a temple made with gold, but flesh. The Church is not a building but a people. Our possessions now serve the purpose of building up God's people both in how they worship and their basic needs fulfilled. We give up that which once satisfied our earthly desires because those desires have been filled by our heavenly God.

Belonging to God's covenant people doesn't just mean that you are not your own, but that your things are not your own. God invites us into a community that practices the same sort of sacrificial generosity He displays to us daily. By embodying a life of sacrificial generosity, we give people a taste of what God has given us in Christ.

When my family received that car, it was a huge blessing and a costly expense. We couldn't believe it. We needed it, and here it was. It was too much for us to gain on our own, but now we held the keys – how much more is this true in Christ, who purchases our salvation with His own blood? What a huge blessing! What a costly expense! We need it, and here it is – so may our giving become as lavish as God's grace, as generous as His love, as we attempt to invite people into covenant relationship with the true Giver of Life.

1. How do you determine what blessings are yours to enjoy or to give?

2. Generosity can be difficult for many reasons, including 1. Poor stewardship 2. Controlling attitude 3. Lack of awareness of needs 4. Lack of funds – What best describes how you might wrestle with generosity?
   What steps do you, or could you, take to overcome this difficulty?

3. Pray that God would make His Church exceedingly generous and hospitable as we care for those in God's covenant people and those outside of it.

COVENANT RESOURCES

TALENTS

DAY TWO

*READ THROUGH EXODUS 35:30-35 +
MATTHEW 25:14-30.*

As you read, write down your observations and ask, *what is the purpose?*

Back in week five, we talked about *calling*. When we think of the word calling, we often associate it with a sort of vocation – "What does God want me to do?" However, when calling is used, it is typically associated with who God is calling you to be, not what He calls you to do. God calls us to find all joy, life, peace, and hope in Christ and what He gives to us, not in what we give to Him.

But there is still good reason to ask, "What does God want me to do for Him?" That question is the natural result of our love for God. When you love someone, it always means more than just strong emotional feelings, but a decision to will their good and act for it.

Here we can see in Exodus and Matthew that God has given people unique giftings and resources to use for His glory. The term 'talent,' often associated with specific skill sets, originates from this story Jesus tells of the talents given. Often times when we focus on what God has called us to do for Him, we focus on spiritual gifts. I don't think this is incorrect, and we should certainly ask how God has spiritually gifted us to glorify Him and edify His people, but often times we miss that our unique talents and precise design have equipped us for a life of service to God.

There are many lists of spiritual gifts throughout scripture (1 Cor. 12, Rom. 12, Eph. 4), but they are not identical or exhaustive. In fact, if we identified a unifying theme throughout them all, it is that what we once could have used to bring more into our own life, we now use to bring spiritual riches into others. Our talents and skills become opportunities to showcase God's glory instead of our own.

Instead of rhetorical skills to win praise, we preach Christ crucified to win converts; instead of our wealth building our kingdom, we provide it to build God's; instead of practicing hospitality to show off our family and home, we practice hospitality to invite others into God's. The Spirit wants to use every part of our life to accomplish God's purpose; the question is, "Are you living your life in ways for that to happen?"

Tim Keller provides a helpful diagnostic to determine God's calling, or vocation, for your life: 1. Am I gifted/skilled? Do you have talents that others around you identify and celebrate? 2. Are you passionate? Do you desire to preach, or serve, or heal, or disciple, or open up your home? 3. Do you have opportunity? Is a door open for you to enjoy your passion and gift in service to His kingdom? If so, chances are that you are being called by God.

What Exodus and Matthew both teach us is that 1. You have been gifted in ways that are meant to be a wonderful blessing to God and His people, and 2. To not use those gifts is squandering a sort of wealth you've been given. To not use your gifts doesn't just take away from your calling and your joy, but others' invitation and their joy.

The responsibility of our calling means we should be wise in what we are engaged in. We can often get caught up in what we desire but not what we are gifted for; in what we are gifted for but have no motivation to do; in what we like but with no open door. Of course, there could be sin issues that are disrupting your motivation or opportunities, but even here, discernment is required, and one of the best ways we discern our calling is through the covenant people.

Paul talks about Timothy and Titus as two individuals he believes have been called for specific tasks, and often those we are closest to can be that guidance for us as well.

The point is, just as with our possessions, our very selves are not our own. We belong to God. We are called to belong to His people. We are called to be a blessing to those who are His. We have a covenant identity that demands all of us, and our joy will be complete when we understand what that identity is in Christ.

1. What are some unique ways you have been gifted? What acts of service come naturally?

2. In what ways do you currently, or could you, use your life to be a blessing to God's people?

3. Pray that God would continue to call and utilize His people to be a blessing to His church and the world and point everyone back to the true 'Blesser' in Christ.

RECAP

Well, you did it. You made it through the devotional and small group study of our covenant relationship with God and its implications for our life. I hope it has benefited you and your development as a Jesus follower. That development comes when our minds are changed to have total faith and trust in Jesus. That development happens when our minds are renewed (Rom. 12:2) and aligned with the vision and will of God. When our beliefs about life become harmonized with what Jesus believes about life, we will not only fulfill our purpose as a human being, but we will enjoy life with the Author of that purpose. We will glorify God and enjoy Him forever. We will have a hope that transforms our lives until God's kingdom comes in full. We will become a part of Gospel proclamation instead of just beneficiaries of it. We will experience completeness in Jesus and find our cup overflows. We hope this study of covenant continues to bring assurance of your life with God and its eternal trajectory.

I invite you to look back through this devotional guide and remember the questions asked, the answers given, and the discussion enjoyed. Perhaps you can dive into some areas of study that you didn't have time for. The point is that this wouldn't become the end of your pursuit, but another lodge along the way that you can come back to and visit.

GOING
DEEPER

GENEROSITY

Jesus teaches those who follow him that giving is better than receiving. This attitude of generosity starts with a commitment to tithe 10% of what God gives us, recognizing that nothing truly belongs to us to hoard. Everything we have is meant to be a blessing. Generosity is a kingdom mindset and a fundamental way God's blessings flow into the world.

SERVING

When we've experienced the goodness of our God, a desire to serve, to engage, and to participate is the natural response. We are not content to simply observe or consume, and we can't imagine keeping the good news of God's love to ourselves. We serve.

We serve in the Church because in God's home we are *hosts* – active participants in the family of God – caring for those in His family and welcoming those who haven't experienced the wholeness in Jesus as we have. We serve in our community and world because we are sent into our neighborhoods, cities, and world to make a Kingdom *impact*. We are the hands and feet of Jesus, called to love and serve all people, showing them the One who loves them most. Scan the code below to find ways to serve with us.

SMALL GROUP
ROUND TABLE

SMALL TALK

Would you rather be unable to speak but able to give away millions of dollars, or be a great preacher but live on $500 a month?

GOOD TALK

What stuck out this week in the study?

What questions or thoughts did you have as you read?

REAL TALK

Go around the room and identify ways you see someone's gifts, abilities, or opportunities to glorify God with their life.

DO SOMETHING DIFFERENT

You are not your own. Our covenant relationship with God and His people has called us out from an isolated, selfishly autonomous life and into an interdependence that enjoys all that we were made for. We have an identity that is in Christ and informs our homes, our marriages, our citizenship, our community, and every part of our life. The purpose of our life is to live and enjoy this relationship at all times, not separating it from work, school, family, and hobbies, but letting it infiltrate every part and bring the fullness of life into those areas. When our lives reflect our covenant identity, they will be enhanced in how we enjoy them, but also how they point us and others to Christ. May we live covenantally and have the assurance that all the promises of God have found their 'yes' in Christ.

PRAYER REQUESTS

OCTOBER 26 / OCTOBER 29, 2023

SERMON NOTES

Catch up or rewatch the sermon
from this week at cco.church/sermons

COVENANT CALLING

1. God's covenant is about God's character.

   Heb. 6: 13-20

   By my word...
      Trust God's word.
   Be with God

2. Trusting God is about needing Him.

   Without Jesus we would drift.
      God is our anchor.

3. Trusting God is about Knowing Him.

NOTES

NOTES

NOTES

NOTES

NOTES

NOTES

NOTES

NOTES

NOTES

NOTES

NOTES

NOTES

NOTES

NOTES

NOTES

NOTES

NOTES

NOTES

NOTES

NOTES

NOTES

NOTES

NOTES

REFERENCE

Part of living life with Jesus in community means celebrating the highs and carrying the lows with one another. Life is messy and we want to help you help each other. Below you will find some useful contacts and resources you can reference to help you love Jesus and each other well.

PASTORAL CARE

When crisis hits, surguries happen, hospital visits become stays or you simply want to talk or pray with someone.

During office hours:
JIM WICKENKAMP
417-673-3945 ext. 113
jim.wickenkamp@cco.church

Outside of office hours:
ROBERT STEVENS
417-673-3945 ext. 141
robert.stevens@cco.church

RIGHT HERE RIGHT NOW

When a finacial or physical need arise, submit a request online or reach out to Allison with questions.

 cco.church/
rhrn

ALLISON STUMP
417-673-3945 ext. 123
allison.stump@cco.church

COUNSELING

To arrange counseling or a one-on-one meeting with a Stephen Minister contact Cindy or schedule an appointment online.

 cco.church/
counseling

CINDY CUTLER
417-673-0090
cindy.cutler@cco.church

DISCIPLESHIP

Need someone to meet with and process through what life with Jesus looks like?

SPENCER HAHN
417-673-3945 ext. 105
spencer.hahn@cco.church

THERESA BARNES
417-673-3945 ext. 159
theresa.barnes@cco.church

PATHWAYS

Find resources to guide you in your time with God. Whether it is developing Bible reading habits or discovering new ways to talk with God, explore this online resource or reach out to Scott with any questions.

 cco.church/
pathways

SCOTT ENSMINGER
417-673-3945 ext. 144
scott.ensminger@cco.church

IMPACT OPPORTUNITIES

Explore ways to serve our community as a small group.

 cco.church/
impact

MAGGIE SCHADE
417-673-3945 ext. 136
maggie.schade@cco.church

FUNERALS & WEDDINGS

To make arrangements for these life-changing events, contact Cindy.

CINDY CUTLER
417-673-0090
cindy.cutler@cco.church

SOURCES

Allison, Gregg R, and John S Feinberg. *Sojourners and Strangers: The Doctrine of the Church*. Wheaton: Crossway, 2012.

Bavinck, Herman. *Wonderful Works of God*. Glenside, PA: Western Seminary Press, 2019.

Beale, G.K. *The Temple and the Church's Mission*, Vol. 17, New Studies in Biblical Theology 17. La Vergne: IVP, 2020.

Gentry, Peter J, and Stephen J Wellum. *Kingdom Through Covenant* (Second Edition). Wheaton: Crossway, 2018.

Horton, Michael. *God of Promise: Introducing Covenant Theology*. Baker Publishing Group, 2009.

Keller, Timothy. *Counterfeit Gods: The Empty Promises of Money, Sex, and Power, and the Only Hope That Matters*. East Rutherford: Penguin Publishing Group, 2009.

Keller, Timothy. *Every Good Endeavor: Connecting Your Work to God's Work*, Redeemer. East Rutherford: Viking, 2012.

Kline, Meredith. *Kingdom Prologue: Genesis Foundations for a Covenantal Worldview*. Eugene, OR: Wipf and Stock Publishers, 2006.

Lioy, Dan. *Axis of Glory: A Biblical and Theological Analysis of the Temple Motif in Scripture*, Vol. 138, Studies in Biblical Literature 138. Bern, Suisse: Peter Lang, 2011.

McGraw, written by Robert Munsch ; illustrated by Sheila. *Love You Forever*, A Firefly Book. Firefly Books, 2018.

"Pokémon Go in a Fractured and Flattened World ," *TheGospelCoalition.Org*, 2016. https://www.thegospelcoalition.org/blogs/trevin-wax/pokemon-go-in-a-fractured-and-flattened-world/.

Renihan, Samuel. *The Mystery of Christ, His Covenant & His Kingdom*. Cape Coral Florida: Founders Press, 2019.

Robertson, O. Palmer. *The Christ of the Covenants*. Phillipsburg, NJ: P Publishing, 1987.

"Statistics of Divorce and Marriage in America," n.d. https://www.cdc.gov/nchs/fastats/marriage-divorce.htm.

Waters, Guy Prentiss, J. Nicholas Reid, John R Muether, Ligon Duncan, Kevin DeYoung, Miles V Van Pelt, John D Wilson, Michael J Kruger, O. Palmer Robertson, and Richard Belcher. *Covenant Theology: Biblical, Theological and Historical Perspectives*. Wheaton: Crossway, 2020.

Watkin, Christopher, and Tim Keller. *Biblical Critical Theory: How the Bible's Unfolding Story Makes Sense of Our Life and Culture*. Grand Rapids: Zondervan Academic, 2022.

Oct. 15 — Church Party
5:30

Covenant — a promise,
an oath between persons,
trustworthiness.

Is a bond.

Made in the USA
Monee, IL
20 August 2023